BEST of
BREED

POODLE

EILEEN GEESON

ACKNOWLEDGEMENTS
The publishers would like to thank the following for help with photography: Eileen Geeson (Janavons), Val and Malcolm Beck;
Steph Holbrook; Lee Cox (Vanitonia); Sandy Vincent (Khyzahra); Claire Nowicka-Price;
Hearing Dogs for Deaf People; Support Dogs; Pets As Therapy.

Cover photo: © Tracy Morgan Animal Photography (www.animalphotographer.co.uk)
Dog featured is Janavons Here Comes Holly, owned by Eileen Geeson.

Pages 2, 103, 104, 105, 134, 144 © Malcolm Beck Photography;
Page 10 © istockphoto.com/Oleg Prikhodko; page 33 © Les Denman; page 34 © Steph Holbrook;
page 39 © istockphoto.com/MichelleMilliman

The British Breed Standard reproduced in Chapter 7 is the copyright of the Kennel Club and published with the club's kind
permission. Extracts from the American Breed Standard are reproduced by kind permission of the American Kennel Club.

THE QUESTION OF GENDER
The 'he' pronoun is used throughout this book instead of the rather impersonal 'it',
but no gender bias is intended.

First published in 2009 by The Pet Book Publishing Company Limited
PO Box 8, Lydney, Gloucestershire GL15 6YD

ISBN
978-1-906305-24-6
1-906305-24-2

Printed and bound in China by PWGS

CONTENTS

Poodle (Feet; Face; Tail; Body); Grooming the show dog
(Mats; Growing hair; To oil or not to oil; the full pupy clip;
The puppy lion; Traditional lion; Continental lion trim);
Summary.

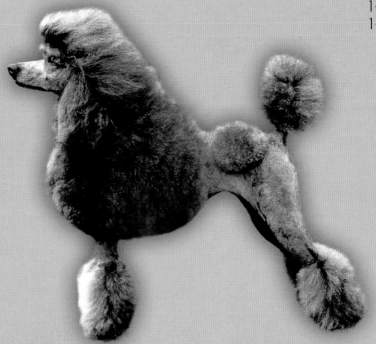

GETTING TO KNOW POODLES

Chapter 1

The Poodle is one of the most intelligent of dogs. Amiable and with a willing temperament that loves to please and make people laugh, there is something in a Poodle's nature that wants people to be happy. This is a highly adaptable breed, both physically and mentally. Eager to cooperate, the essentially light boned Poodle has excellent manoeuvrability and problem-solving skills that make him a companion *par excellence*.

This is a biddable, trustworthy breed cherished the world over. As a companion one could not wish for a more devoted friend or a stauncher supporter. Their natural inclination is to be sweet and charming, kind and tender-hearted. Cry, and he cries with you, laugh and he is ecstatic.

Here is a breed of dog that will happily accompany his owner on a shopping trip, will pose for photographs with models, will act the clown in a circus, yet who will lead the blind, aid the hard of hearing, and be a home help to the aged and those with disabilities. He will perform high standards of obedience exercises and perform to perfection at top levels in working, utility and service needs.

OVERCOMING STEREOTYPES

Unfortunately, the Poodle has had something of an image crisis. The unusual trimming of the show Poodle, brought about by tradition (see Chapter Two), has led to the less well informed deciding that the Poodle is nothing more than a powder-puff,

The elaborate style of trimming Poodles for the show ring has led to misconceptions about the breed.

THE THREE VARIETIES

The Standard Poodle.

The Miniature Poodle.

The Toy Poodle.

devoid of brain capacity. This misconception has been made worse by publicity-seeking individuals who dandify the breed to extremes, going as far as colouring the coat in shocking colours, such as green, pink, and lilac.

All this does a great disservice to the breed. Those prepared to ignore the stereotypes and really get to know this clever, versatile breed, will discover that, far from being a freak product of canine evolution, the Poodle is actually a loyal, intelligent and fun canine, capable of being an ideal family pet or a successful working dog.

VARIETIES

Poodles come in different sizes, from 10 inches (25 cm) or less, to as tall as 28 inches (71 cm) or more at the shoulder. There are three varieties:

- **The Standard Poodle:** The largest of the Poodle varieties is usually between 22 and 26 inches (56 and 66 cm), but can be outside this range. The official Kennel Club Breed Standard gives the size as being over 15 inches (38 cm) at the shoulder.

- **The Miniature Poodle:** This variety has been around equally as long as the larger Standard Poodle. Although no longer required by the Kennel club to be measured in the show ring, the Poodle Council still insist their judges measure the Miniature and Toy Poodle to keep a check on the size limit. The Miniature Poodle should be between 11 and 15 inches (28 and 38 cms)

- **The Toy Poodle:** The smallest of the varieties, the Toy Poodle is 11 inches (28 cms) or under.

The Toy Poodle, the Miniature Poodle or the Standard Poodle may all be varieties of the same breed, but it is true to say there is a difference between them. Their size contributes to their ability to successfully implement specific tasks. For example, the Toy Poodle, however adaptable of spirit, is not physically suited to guiding the blind. Neither is the Miniature Poodle. However, both these sizes can be used to aid the hard of hearing.

The Poodle can live to a ripe old age, so anyone thinking about taking on a Poodle (or any dog, for that matter), should consider it a long-term commitment. I have had many Standards live to 16 years. Some of my friends have 17-18 year old Miniature and Toy Poodles. I believe some Poodles have reached 20 years or more.

NEW TO THE BREED

Some people acquire their first Poodle because of his coat. Dog lovers who are allergic to dog hair purchase their first Poodle because he has a wool coat rather than normal moulting hair, which therefore does not induce allergy. However, having lived with a Poodle for only a short time they realise the intrinsic qualities of

the breed and become hooked; they will never change their breed for another. If you haven't actually owned a Poodle, don't knock it, for you know nothing!

Others may acquire a Poodle by default. Sometimes a relative has passed on a Poodle to another member of the family because of ill health or death. Some people love the look of the breed because they are as cuddly as lambs and just as funny to watch when the mood takes them to display their sense for the ridiculous. Some new Poodle owners have met a friend's dog, admired his outstanding qualities and then acquired one of their own.

Whether you have owned Poodles before, or are new to the breed, this is a delightful breed that has something to offer everyone. Once you own one,

prepare to be captivated for life. Poodle owners rarely change to another breed of dog; indeed, they usually end up with another, and then another…

PHYSICAL CHARACTERISTICS

The Poodle has many looks, but beneath the hair the basic structure is sound, square, and well balanced. The Poodle is characterised by an easy, flowing movement, with the capability, when mature, to jump, twist and turn with amazing mobility – hence the breed's great success within the world of obedience, agility and other aspects of performance, such as dancing to music (see Chapter 6).

The breed should never appear exaggerated in construction. He is finely boned but strong. His

The basic structure of the Poodle is sound, characterised by easy, flowing movement.

A Poodle will tune into your feelings, as well as communicating his own moods and emotions.

carriage is elegant and proud. His temperament is happy, spirited and good-natured. The eyes, almond shaped and preferably dark, show liveliness, intelligence and kindness.

The fact that the Poodle does not shed its coat makes it a desirable breed for those sensitive to dog hair. Allergy sufferers, asthmatics for example, can quite reliably own a Poodle without causing severe reaction. The down side to this, if one wants to look for one, is that the Poodle must be groomed regularly and bathed and clipped of his excess hair every four to six weeks to keep the coat in good, healthy condition, and this costs money unless the owner can undertake this task himself. Having a wool-type coat that does not moult, the hair can be styled or sculptured into many different trims to suit the requirements of the owner.

POODLE TEMPERAMENT

The Poodle is extremely people oriented. He is a social creature, most comfortable when part of the social 'pack'. The Poodle is a family dog that loves his friends, is tolerant and amiable towards visitors (unless they have shown him distaste), easy to train and willing.

The changing emotions of the Poodle can be seen in the different facial expressions he uses to communicate (most obvious when the face is shaved). The extraordinary changes, which express emotion, action, enthusiasm, fun, sadness or stress, are observed with amazement and great amusement and interest to those with the ability to understand.

The emotions of owners are often mirrored by their Poodle facial expressions. The Poodle can smile with the softness of love or the sparkle of an imp. He can look very sympathetic when we feel low or sad and show sadness

10

when we cry. Arguments and shouting will cause him to show apprehension and fear. This is a breed very in tune with human emotion.

The Poodle is possessed with a nature of utmost loyalty. In the book *Travels with Charlie – in search of America* John Steinbeck, tells how his Standard Poodle, Charlie, travels with him on his journey. Thought to be the gentlest creature imaginable and the greatest coward on earth, when suddenly faced with a huge mountain bear he tries to defend his owner. The Poodle is courageous when fully mature and will warn off intruders with a magnificent bellow of the lungs. He will greet a stranger on the doorstep in a friendly fashion if the human of the house seems welcoming, but is equally capable of grumbling and pulling faces of discontent if the opposite is true. Because of this free thinking nature, it is vital that anyone thinking of taking on a Poodle (or a dog of any breed, for that matter), is able to position themselves as leader of the family 'pack'. This means taking control in a calm, assertive (not aggressive) and confident manner.

The Poodle is also a great problem solver. Without adequate training he can run circles around his human family, but in the right home with disciplined, loving owners, the Poodle makes a wonderful family pet, who will play happily with children and adults who treat him with mutual respect. He will join in the fun of dressing up

Katie Boyle with her Poodle Daisy May: Once you have owned a Poodle, no other breed will do.

with children, enjoy a walk in the sunshine or a race in the snow, or perform to a high standard in the show ring or any competition.

I must warn prospective owners that this is a breed that loves to have fun. A friend once spent two hours planting out bedding plants, only to find that in two minutes flat the lot were retrieved and placed into little piles on the patio. Be warned, this breed does like to dig. Poodles were, after all, used to seek out truffles growing beneath the surface of the ground. And woe betide any moles tunnelling in the garden; their fate is not

good. The only trouble is a few deep holes will be dug in the excavation required to get the mole.

Poodles seem to have a sixth sense. I have often thought or said I must wake up at a certain time and one of my dogs will start poking me at this time. A friend of mine frequently says her Poodle knows her more than she knows herself! So often one only has to think about going for a walk and the Poodles are up and waiting for the leads to be put on, or for me to grab the car keys. When I think about taking the balls out into the paddock to

Poodles are fun lovers and will join in all the family activities.

throw, they are waiting by the cupboard where the outside balls are kept before I have time to move.

THE RIGHT HOME

Having said that the Poodle makes a wonderful companion and is highly adaptable, he is not, however, suitable for everyone. The right owner will take the time and trouble to get to know the breed and establish him/herself as leader.

The Poodle will frequently voice excitement when friends approach or other dogs and humans join his company. This vocal response doesn't usually last more than a few minutes after the arrival of the visitor. Puppies learn to bark from other dogs. Excessive barking is the result of isolation and insufficient or inadequate training.

Because of the Poodle's unique coat, the breed is sometimes considered to be nothing more than a couch potato or cream puff. Yes, the Poodle (of all sizes) loves his spot on the sofa, with his head resting in your lap, but, the Poodle person – those aware of the real character of the breed – prefer the Poodle for his intelligence, extreme loyalty, good temper, sense of fun, and versatility. Hence, year after year we see all sizes of the Poodle performing great feats at Crufts, and other famous events.

A life-long friendship will develop for those who love and cherish the Poodle. The Poodle is happiest when living as a free member of the family, in the family home at all times. Isolation will result in the development of antisocial behaviour and behavioural problems.

POODLES AND CHILDREN

Poodles adapt very well to family life. Children must be part of everyday life to the dog we want to keep as a friend and companion. Socialisation with children is relatively easy with a bit of thought. Even if you don't have children a pup can be introduced to children outside schools, with the permission of the parents, or taken along to Garden Centres where invariably there are children running about. Other good sources are the supermarket car park and car boot sales. If we fail our Poodles in this primary education we will invite opposition from those on the wrong end of a badly raised dog.

POODLES AND OTHER PETS

In the same way, the Poodle socialised with other pets will readily take to them as friends and live in perfect harmony with them. Even where early socialisation is neglected, a Poodle can be quickly acclimatised to other pets. Success lies in the way the introduction is handled (see Chapter 6).

EXERCISE & COMPANIONSHIP

The Poodle is an adaptable breed and will be happy living in a small caravan, in a town, or in a country estate, provided he is well loved and given adequate exercise to run off excess energy, particularly when he is a young adult. Puppies sleep a lot, but still need to be given adequate time to play and learn. The main priority for this breed is his need to belong. He will adore family members, especially children, and needs lengthy interaction with people on a daily basis. The Poodle will not be happy in a home where he is left on his own for hours each day.

Dogs were not designed to spend half their lives in a cage. Any Poodle shut in a cage for too long can become quite neurotic when released unless very careful consideration has been given to cage socialisation. I vehemently disagree with caging for any reason other than use as a den, at shows, for safety reasons, and for restriction following surgery. Your home should be your Poodle's home, and he will respect this if you establish yourself as pack leader. For more information on using a crate or cage appropriately, see Chapter 6.

Because the Poodle loves to be a companion he will relish trips out in the car to visit other people, to go shopping, or for exercise in new places such as walks, parks and the beach. For this reason they are a popular breed with those who like to caravan. It is a good idea to get a puppy accustomed to riding in the car as soon as possible. For this most puppies are simply put on the back seat of the car on a blanket, with a seat belt if preferred. Some people prefer to contain their dogs in the back of the car, but unless this is a car with a large, roomy boot, this can be cruel. Also be careful about leaving your dog in the car in hot weather. Dogs can become

Once mutual respect has been established, a Poodle will develop a very special bond with younger members of the family.

overheated and die in a surprisingly short amount of time.

Those wanting a low-energy dog with no sense of adventure should never entertain owning this breed. Ideally, the Poodle should be given at least one walk a day. An adult will walk several miles happily. A puppy should be restricted to several short walks, increasing in length as he grows.

He will also enjoy other forms of exercise. For example, most Poodles love to dance. At home, when we put on the music for a spot of rock-n-roll, our dogs love to join in, jumping for joy.

TRAINABILITY
A well-trained Poodle of any size is an asset to any household. With such intelligence this is a fairly easy goal to achieve. The

Poodles are adaptable dogs, as long as they receive sufficient mental stimulation and human companionship.

more effort put into training, the greater the rewards. If the owner/trainer gets the signals and communication right, the Poodle will learn almost as quickly as clicking the fingers. He is bright and intelligent and only fear or heavy-handedness will slow his progress.

A Poodle suffering the effects of neglect or over-indulgence will react accordingly – sometimes going as far as chewing valuables, and, in extreme cases, fighting and biting. Thankfully this is very unusual. Unless a Poodle is sick, you can attribute bad or uncharacteristic behaviour to the owner. Indeed, it is unusual to find a Poodle with an attitude problem that has not been induced by his rearing. Lack of consistency is the main cause of problem behaviour, such as allowing the dog on the furniture when he is clean, but not when he has muddy paws. Some owners mistakenly train their

Poodle at cross-purposes. For example, tiny Toy Poodles may be hugged to the bosom and not allowed to socialise, especially in the crucial socialisation period of 3-16 weeks of age (see Chapter 6). It is within this period that the interaction and contact with other dogs and humans will have a permanent and essential effect on a puppy that will stay with him for the rest of his life. No Toy Poodle thinks he is small!

No dog is naughty. He may be untrained or acting naturally in a way that has developed because his owners forgot that a dog is not a human being and does not have the capability or reasoning power that belongs to the human. Dogs that mess up the house, take things you didn't intend them to have (you call it stealing) dig holes in the flower bed, chase cats, and urinate on the sofa, are purely and simply acting normally. It is our job, our responsibility, to train the dog to

urinate where we want. It is up to us to distract the dog from chewing our valuables and apply his inherent lust for exercising his jaw and cleaning his teeth on subjects we choose for him, such as raw bones and safe dog chews. It is our responsibility to take our pet out for a brisk morning walk, so that he is not left with excess energy that could turn to boredom and destructiveness.

Poodles are very quick to learn. In 1880 Dr. Gorden Stables said of the Poodle "I must not forget two lovely and gentle-tempered pets I once possessed. I got them from France and French was the only language they knew. My accent was abominable – so 'Gamin', the dog, told me – but as I chose not to go to school again to please a Poodle, I proceeded to teach them English, and they understood all I said in six weeks. Dogs are good linguists. I had one once to whom I spoke in English, Latin, Greek, Gaelic, and good broad Scotch. My dead and gone Champion, 'Theodore Nero', hadn't resided in Wales with me over six weeks before he knew all the servants said to him." Their intuitive understanding of people means they can pick up as much from your tone of voice and body language as the actual word or phrase you use.

My belief is that the happiest Poodle owners, and the most well-balanced Poodles, are those who 'do things' together. A good way to start your Poodle's socialisation and training is to attend training classes. The

Poodle will enjoy himself and conduct himself well with other dogs and people when suitably treated. This is a breed that wants to please, loves to be praised, and derives great satisfaction in getting things right, so when things go wrong, it is usually down to the owner's lack of intuition or impatience. Finding a good training class can avoid this.

THE VERSATILE POODLE

No matter what size, the Poodle is one of the most versatile breeds in the world. In the Peninsular war (1808-1814) it was a Poodle that carried the French colours to safety when the standard-bearer was mortally wounded, and so it was that he became the hero dog of the first French Republic. Today, the Poodle has life-long devotees who admire him for many different reasons: whether that is the elegance and glamour of the show dog, the helping paws of the home help, therapy dog, guide dog or hearing dog; the skills of the search-and-rescue dog; the talent and agility of the competition dog; or the loving nature of the trusted family pet, who invariably puts a smile on your face with his natural antics and willingness to please.

The Poodle's special intelligence, adaptability and ability to bond with his owner, makes him a

This is a breed with a sound temperament; behavioural problems are generally caused by over-indulgence on the part of the owner.

perfect candidate for various categories of assistance dog. So much so, The Canine Companions for Independence and the Lions Foundation of Canada both have a breeding programme, which includes Standard Poodles as assistance dogs.

DOGS FOR THE DISABLED

The Poodle works very well as an assistance dog helping people with disabilities. One person

who is very aware of the advantages of training her Poodle to help is Rosemary McGarry from Farnham in Hampshire. Rosemary has a Standard Poodle she calls OJ, which is short for Odd Jobs.

Being disabled, Rosemary first taught OJ to climb up on a chair, then on to a table for grooming purposes. He quickly learned to turn himself to assist Mary with all angles of his coat brushing.

OJ starts his day by passing Rosemary her clothes as she sits on her bed, then he carries anything required downstairs for her, sometimes doing two or three trips. He pulls clothes out of the washing machine and picks up pegs that Rosemary may drop during her effort to get them on the dryer. OJ fetches shoes, the hairbrush, keys, etc. He will pick up the ringing telephone and 'talk' into it before bringing it to Rosemary. Life for Rosemary has certainly been made easier with the aid of her remarkable, if somewhat unusual, home help.

THERAPY DOGS

In many countries there is a registered charity that runs an organisation designed to utilise pets as therapy dogs. There are a growing number of Poodles

15

Murphy works as a therapy dog, bringing comfort to many.

joining the list of dogs that are trained for the use of aiding and stimulation of the physically and mentally impaired. Members of therapy groups take their registered Poodles along to visit the elderly living in homes, to nursing homes, to visit children in schools for the advantage of education and to special needs school for the mentally and physically disabled. They also visit hospices and private homes where visits from the dog do much to benefit the health and mental wellbeing of people who love dogs but cannot hope to own one. Some autistic children find it far easier to communicate and interact with a therapy dog than with another human.

Therapy Poodles are gentle and under control. They are confident around strangers and reliable in a sometimes fraught atmosphere. Sometimes they will perform tricks. My own therapy Poodles have done this. They throw a ball in the air and catch it, bow down on their fronts with bottom in air, talking doggy language that some autistic children seem to understand. Two of my Poodles, Rainbow and Beryl, had a habit, stimulated by response from very young children, to sit on a chair around a table to join in a tea party. These two dogs have even queued up at the play-shop to help purchase items when the children are play-taught how to shop. This causes tremendous amusement and encourages interaction.

I know that my Standard Poodles are even-tempered, but when I was first asked to visit a school for children with learning difficulties, I must admit to being slightly apprehensive. Neither the dogs nor me had had any experience with these special children. I took two of my Pro-Dog registered Standard Poodles, Rainbow and Denim, along for them to make friends with the children. It only took a few minutes for me to realise these dogs were far better adjusted mentally to cope with this unusual situation than I had given them credit for.

The disabilities of some children, especially those with autism, force them to live in a world of their own. It was

hoped, in time, a bond would be cemented between the dogs and the children. In fact, a friendship sprang with immediate effect. The class of 13 to 15-year-old children were soon smiling from ear to ear when Rainbow and Denim nudged them for attention. We had introduced the dogs during the tea break and it was only moments before Denim and Rainbow were sharing biscuits with the laughing children. Even an autistic boy who liked to keep to his own corner found himself interested in these strange, furry dogs.

Having established a good relationship with the older children the dogs were then introduced to a class of younger children, between five and seven years of age. Some of these children had never had any contact with a dog at all. They were very frightened, but the Poodle who is socially trained is very clever at winning friends. With a gentleness one had to see to believe, Denim approached an almost hysterically nervous child by crawling along the floor on his belly. At first this little girl screamed in horror, but soon she became curious of this wriggling ball of fluff and gingerly, with encouragement from me, reached out to feel it. This frightened youngster, named Emma, developed a particular and special bond with the dogs and changed from being fearful and apprehensive into a happy and confident little girl, the active therapy achieving its purpose.

Hearing Dog Mack.

Hearing Dog Blossom.

HEARING DOGS

Hearing dogs are trained to perform a variety of tasks to help their deaf owners, such as making their owners aware of the telephone ringing or the ringing of a doorbell. Many deaf people are now more independent and experience a more confident attitude when assisted by a hearing dog.

The black Standard Poodle 'Glennie' proved to be a vital link for Margaret Tovey, in her job as a senior radiographer in a busy X-ray unit at Weston General Hospital. Glennie's job included alerting his deaf owner to telephone calls, the chemical mixer and pager, and to the fire alarm – as well as the tea trolley. On duty round the clock Glennie became the 'ears' of Margaret. The hope is that more local authorities will recognise the power of assistance dogs, and in particularly Poodles – with their hygienic non-moulting hair – and will be encouraged to employ them as unpaid, special aid/pets for disabled people.

SEARCH AND RESCUE DOGS

Poodles can be trained for search and rescue services, which include water search dogs, wilderness search dogs, avalanche search dogs and disaster search dogs. These special dogs have to undergo individual training with the emphasis on the particular requirement.

Poodles seem to have an exceptional ability to react to alarm signals, even where specialised training has not been given. When mother-to-be Catherine Farthing lay in agony after falling and breaking her ankle during an evening walk in dense woodland, she found herself stranded on a steep slope 15ft from the edge of a fast flowing river, which drowned out her cries for help.

Gus, a seven year old Standard Poodle owned by Maggie and Charles Piper, who lived 200 yards away from the river, alerted his owners to the desperate situation when he pricked up his ears and then starting barking and frantically pawing the door. Maggie and Charles let Gus out and followed him. Maggie heard faint cries for help as Gus led her and Charles across a bridge. "I crossed the

GUIDE DOGS

Standard Poodle Crosby, named after the star Bing Crosby, went through rigorous training at the Redbridge Guide Dog for the Blind Centre. Along with his litter brother Corky, he passed out as a fully-fledged Guide Dog and Crosby became Christopher Collis's link with the seeing world. Christopher had no previous experience of Poodles, and it was only on his first introduction to his allotted Guide Dog that he discovered Crosby was a Standard Poodle.

Guide Dogs always prove interesting to the general public, Crosby attracts attention; people are fascinated about him being a Poodle. They are far more accustomed to seeing Labradors and Golden Retrievers as Guide Dogs for the Blind. However, the Poodle's intelligence and even temperament, along with the low allergy risk of his coat, are great attributes for a guide dog. Crosby's special aptitude came to the fore when his training had to suit Christopher's disabilities and he was taught to lead his master from the right instead of the usual left.

Asked if there were any problems at all working with a Poodle, Christopher recalls: "To begin with Crosby was a bit too interested in pigeons in our precinct, but after a few words of firm encouragement to leave, Crosby came to ignore the birds!"

Grooming need not present too much of a problem when the coat is trimmed to a sensible length for management. Probably the only down side to the Guide Dog Association using the Poodle is that the coat care does mean extra expense for them.

first bridge and heard another 'Help me'." After crossing another bridge in the difficult woodland terrain, Gus led his owners to find Catherine as she lay in agony upon the ground. Catherine had broken her ankle in three parts and could not be moved with ease in her delicate condition.

Charles Piper dashed home to raise the alarm while Maggie and Gus stayed with Catherine until the paramedics arrived. Because of the difficult terrain and her serious condition, Catherine was lifted by helicopter to Yeovil Hospital where she made a full recovery – thanks to Gus.

SUPPORT/SEIZURE ALERT DOGS

Dogs for many of us, are lifelines. We cannot, or do not want, to live without our faithful friends. And why should we? Dogs support us in many ways, each deserving credit and respect. One such dog is Milo, the first Standard Poodle to qualify as a Support Dog.

Hannah Baker was only six years of age when she developed epilepsy. She began dropping things for no apparent reason, and black lines suddenly appeared across her drawings as seizures caused her hand to shoot across the paper. After several scans, Hannah was diagnosed with a non-malignant brain tumour and over the next few years her seizures gradually grew worse until she was suffering as many as 80 a day, of varying degrees of severity. Hannah's epilepsy was so incapacitating she was virtually housebound, requiring 24 hour care. Simple tasks like taking a shower required her to sing constantly, to alert her family and carers that she was okay. As a child she had to sleep in a double bed to prevent her from falling out and injuring herself. Accidents, such as breaking her jaw in three places, became commonplace.

An operation to remove the

THE FIRST POODLES

Chapter 2

The Poodle may have originated in France, Germany or Russia, but while many countries like to claim the eminent and striking Poodle as theirs, there is no evidence to substantiate the breed's origin to one country or another. Indeed it was reported that dogs similar to the Poodle were seen in many parts of the Continent around the same time, from 1553.

Originally used as a retrieving/hunting dog, constantly in and out of rivers and lakes, the forerunners of today's Poodle had dense waterproof coats. This was an impediment and was trimmed accordingly, to enable freedom of movement in the water while leaving enough hair for protection against the cold and dense undergrowth. These dogs were, and are still, not the fickle lap dogs that their coiffure looks will have us believe. This type of dog was used as a gun/flushing dog in East Anglia in the 17th Century and can be referred to as the 'prototype Poodle'.

THE FIRST POODLES
It is stated in early Poodle books, such as *Our Friend the Poodle* by Rowland Johns (1848), that the larger Poodle was preferred in Russia, while in France and Germany the slightly smaller dog was preferred. Documentation and drawings show there were variations in size very early on. Today, we still have what is classed as the larger and smaller Standard Poodle. Height restrictions in the Toy Poodle and Miniature Poodle have maintained size within desired limits.

The Poodle has always been a very cosmopolitan breed, being popular in many countries, such as Greece, Spain, Italy, Britain and in later years, America and Canada. Research has not, as yet, given a clear indication of who was originally responsible for crossing the first selected breeds to produce what was to become the pure-bred Poodle. One way we can attempt to chart development is by looking at art history – both pictorial and the artists' own accounts and opinions.

THE POODLE IN ART
The first authentic representation of the Poodle in art appears to be that of a clipped Miniature in the famous tapestry, whose permanent home is in the museum at Cluny (France). The tapestry is one of a series known as *The Lady with the Unicorn*. The marginal decorations show the hindquarters and half the body of (say the experts) a Lion-clipped Poodle. If correct, this is historical evidence that the Poodle was in those days (about

EARLY POODLES

Boye was owned by Prince Rupert of the Rhine, a Royalist leader in the English Civil War (1625-1649). Boye was killed in the Battle of Marston Moor (1644), when Rupert suffered a heavy defeat at the hands of the combined forces of the Scottish Covenanters and the English Parliamentarians. Prince Rupert was reputed to be heartbroken.

The Poodle has always been a very cosmopolitan breed. This pet was photographed in France around 1885.

1510) a recognised companion of the great Ladies of France, that the Miniature variety was in existence, and that clipping has been practised for at least 450 years. In his research, Johns set out to find some pictorial representations of the Poodle in past centuries and discovered Basil Ionides, the husband of Nellie Ionides of the Vulcan kennels, had a collection of prints that were significant in his categorising the history of the breed for his book.

The earliest print in the collection is dated 1516 and is an allegorical engraving after Raphael, presumed to be the Roman goddess Aurora gazing into the blinding rays of the sun, while at her feet stands a Miniature Poodle. Also in the collection there were engravings of French origin. One is descriptive of the days of James I (1603-25), entitled *The Five Senses* – based upon tapestry designs of the early Stuart period and shows a clipped Poodle.

Engravings of the period 1770-1800 depict Poodles of various sizes. There is one showing a parti-colour French Barbet (Poodle), the colouring said to have been put on by hand and showing the head markings and a well-defined saddle of dark brown.

Sir Edwin Landseer (1803-1873) shows a large white Poodle type with smaller Toy dogs in his *Trial by Jury,* which is depicted on various postcards, tea trays and other collectables from the Devonshire Collection, Chatsworth, Derbyshire.

The 19th century witnessed

the golden age of the caricaturists, who rejoiced in delineating the foibles of high society. Their artistry provides evidence of the Poodle being a prominent feature in society life, in both France and England. Certainly the breed appeared as a symbol of wealth.

Some most striking pictures, of which I have one, are those by French artists drawing from life the groomers of the day clipping and trimming the Poodles of Paris before and after the Revolution. A coloured print entitled *Tendreuses des Chiens* shows two women in aprons, sitting under large umbrellas, trimming Poodles as they await more custom on the pavement by the side of the River Seine. These were the canine beauty parlours or grooming salons of the 18th-century.

Another picture depicts a sausage maker with a hopeful looking Poodle standing near his stove. Also shown is a French coloured print of this period of brown, clipped Poodles, being used for duck shooting. A coloured print engraved after a painting of the English cartoonist Henry Banbury, printed in 1803 by Brown of Pall Mall, London, is an interesting portrayal of an itinerant family of entertainers taking the road to Savoy. They are carrying their musical instruments and being led along by an enormous performing bear, straining at his chain to keep up with a Poodle with a Lion clip who gaily leads the way.

A print was issued after the Peninsular war entitled *Hyde Park*

The clipped Poodle became a symbol of fashion and wealth.

which shows Lord Worcester walking a Poodle named Sacho, whom he adopted at the battle of Salamanca (1812) when the faithful Poodle was found lying on the grave of his master, a lieutenant in the defeated French army. The Poodle's close association with the army is exemplified in a print depicting the entry into Algiers (1830). In this print a Poodle named Mitraille proudly leads the cavalry through the main gateway (well bedecked with several human heads) into the conquered stronghold of the pirates and slave traders.

The devotion of the Poodle is

typified in a colour print showing Louis Philippe (Louis XV111, last King of France) fleeing with his wife from the fury of the Republicans; their only companion through their flight in the snow is a Poodle, according to Johns in his depiction of *Artists Tell Us The Truth.*

WHAT CAN HISTORY TELL US?
As well as charting the general development of the Poodle into the dog we know today, looking at historical references can provide us with information about the origins of the three different varieties of Poodle and the emergence of the various

clipping traditions. The print after Raphael demonstrates that, as early as 1516, the size of the poodle is depicted as small – miniature in fact. We can, therefore, conclude that the different sizes are not a product of clever, selective breeding of modern day breeders. The Toy variety may well have come later, but from the 15th century we see both the smaller and large Poodle depicted in art. From 1770-1800 Poodles of all sizes are mentioned in literature.

Clipping of the early Poodle, said Gervase Markham in his book of 1655 *Hungers Prevention: or The Whole Arte of Fowling by Water and Land,* was necessary because

> '... these Water Dogges naturally are ever laden with haire on the hinder parts; nature as it were labouring to defend that part most, which is continually to be employed in the most extremity, and because the hinder parts are ever deeper in the water then the fore-parts, therefore nature hath given them the greatest armour of haire to defend the wett and coldness; yet this defence in the summer time by the violence of the heate of the sunne, and the

We can learn about the development of the Poodle from its depictions in art.

> greatness of the Dogges labour is very noysome and troublesome, and not onely maketh him sooner faint and give over his sport, but also makes him by his overheating, more subject to take the mange...'

Perhaps the origin of the traditional Lion clip came when Markham reported that the heavy coat of the Poodle made him swim *'less nimbly and it was essential for the benefit of the Poodle*

in his success as a water dog to shave the hind parts'. Shaving the complete body of the Poodle was not recommended, as protection of the heart, lungs and chest *'Ayre he shall frize'* was essential.

Historical art and literature suggest that the clipping/shaving/ trimming of poodles has been practised for nearly five centuries. The Lion clip as we know it today (historically referred to as the French clip in some instances) has been favoured in the show ring and in fashion for hundreds of years.

It appears from artistic impressions that canine beauty parlours of the 18th century were alfresco. It is believed that, in France, the shaving of poodles, as distinct from close clipping, was widely practised.

The Lion clip was depicted everywhere, especially during the reign of Louis XV (1723-1775). Early drawings usually show the Poodle with a large mane of hair covering the neck, shoulders and chest, long fringes on the ears and a profuse top-knot, invariably tied up with a coloured ribbon so that the owners could distinguish their dogs when they worked in reeds.

Initially, the Poodle's coat was clipped for purely practical reasons.

The traditional Lion clip has found favour for hundreds of years.

THE BREED STANDARD

Poodles seem to have been recognised by the Kennel club almost since its foundation. Five Poodles appear in the Kennel Club Stud Book of 1875. Stud book entries for the Poodle grow year on year until, in 1883, they are divided by sex for the first time, with 11 dogs and five bitches being registered.

The Poodle Club was founded in 1876. The original Poodle Breed Standard was drawn up on December 16th 1885. The Poodle Club applied for KC recognition in 1896 (this was not a requirement in the early years of the KC). The first Poodle to be awarded the title of Champion, in 1890, was Ch. Achilles (born 1886, bred by MR. Kemp). There arose a great controversy over whether corded and curly Poodles should be classes separately and the Curly/Corded 'schism' was formalised by the founding of the Curly Poodle Club in 1900 by Miss Brunker. Unfortunately, records of this club became another casualty of World War II when they were lost as the result of bombing in 1943.

In 1910, according to The Poodle by Clara Bowring and Alida Monroe, the Secretary of the Kennel Club wrote to the Poodle Club asking its opinion on various points connected with the breed. The Club replied that in the opinion of its Committee Miniature Poodles should be measured on a table in the Show Ring.

In 1911, 16 Miniature Poodles were registered, listed as from Miss Millie Brunker's Whippendell Cachet, Whippendell Cabillat, Whippendell Turqu; Miss Newall's Manikin of Ellingham and Mrs Cobbiold's white Alresford Powder Puff were amongst these. Miss Brunker was breeding and showing her large Poodles and Miniatures.

The current Breed Standard is the result of Kennel Club liaison with the Poodle Breed Clubs.

The coat was clipped close on the hindquarters, rear end, from end of ribs, over loins and buttock and thigh. Both front and hind legs were clipped close to wrist and hock joint where hair was left to the toe.

THE 20TH CENTURY

From 1918 the popularity of the Poodle increased steadily and was not unduly affected during the 1939-45 war years, although with the coming of the war many breeders had to severely restrict their breeding programme.

MINIATURES AND TOYS

The popularity of the different sizes of Poodle tends to wax and wane over the years. Currently the Standard Poodle has the highest number of entries in the show ring, followed by the Toy Poodle and then the Miniature. Before we had measuring in the ring, some Miniature Poodles were very large. An early Poodle (1904) called Mowgli, bred by Colonel Chapman, did a lot of winning. He was sired by a dog by the name of Piccolo and his dam was Frou Frou. He stood 17 inches in height. For some years now the Miniature Poodle being registered must be born of Miniature parents, and the same applies to the Toy Poodle. Size is therefore more reliable.

The earlier Toy Poodle was frequently referred to as being rather 'thick of skull'. This has greatly improved in recent years and we now see some beautiful, typical heads on all three sizes as well as nicely constructed, outgoing Poodles of excellent temperament and great character.

The Braeval (Mrs. Phillis

Austin-Smith) and the Piperscroft (Mrs Grace Boyd) Miniatures, and later the Montfleuri (Mrs Howard Price), were significant kennels that appear in the majority of pedigrees. The Manerheads line came into the Braeval line from a sire called Harwee. Also noted as significant were the Firebrave-Chievely lines. Alida Monro bred an important litter that contained Firebrave Cupidon and Ch. Barty of Piperscroft, who was registered by Mrs Boyd. Later we saw the Bidabo, Aspen, Tranchant and Lochranza come to the fore with many excellent dogs.

Toy Poodles were generally known to be descendants of the two sizes of larger Poodle. However, many breeders, including Lady Stainer with her Seahorses kennel, believe the tiny truffle-digging dogs of France and Germany were responsible for this important size. Mrs Anne Hall of the Wychwood kennel imported some of these tiny dogs from France and Germany, as well as America.

Ch. Barsbrae Branslake Darty, Branslake Diablo and his son, Ch. Trespetite Jansteen Black Wings had an influence on the British Toys, with Diablo siring many Toy Champions. The offspring were noted for their classical heads, almond eyes, and refinement. Later the Tuttlebees,

Vulcan Champagne Cliquot, born 1934.
Photo: Thomas Fall.

Montmartres, and Tophills had great success along with kennels such as the Petitbruns who are noted as primarily breeding down from their own Miniatures.

STANDARDS
In 1934 Mrs Nellie Ionides founded a kennel in England that proved to be the most historic and significant. Nellie Ionides was the breeder of a few different breeds of dog, and when she added Standard Poodles to her kennels she added Champagne to their name. Her first sire and first Champion was Vulcan Champagne Pommery, whom she purchased from the Berkham kennels. According to records the first black Standard born at Vulcan (16.02.1938) was Vulcan Black Varnish, by Nunsoe Alaternus out of Skyhigh Sheen. In 1934 Vulcan Champagne Cliquot was born, bred by Mrs Walsh. Vulcan Champagne Cliquot, was a cream descending

from creams and apricots and was one of the first dogs to be shown in the ring coming from Vulcan Champagne. He never became a Champion but his progeny proved themselves most worthy.

The main kennels reported to maintain the Standard Poodle during the Second World War, were the Piperscroft, Nunsoe, Rathnally and the Vulcan Champagne. In the early post-war years, some of the kennels at the forefront of Standard Poodle breeding and exhibiting were Nunsoe (Jane Lane), Beechover (Miss R Gregory), Frenches (Mrs R Price-Jones), Peaslake (Mrs Hilliard), Piperscroft (Mrs Boyd), and of course, the Vulcan Champagne (Mrs Ionides and Shirley Walne). Some other names of consequence were Mrs Fife-Fails, Mrs English, Miss Hocken, Mrs Skeaping, Miss Bowring and Mrs Monroe, breeding different sizes.

The Frenches and the Peaslake kennels both evolved from mostly Vulcan Champagne stock. Frenches and the Vulcan Champagne dogs dominated the show ring, producing many Champions. Rita Price-Jones had four bitches of different colours from the Vulcan kennels. The late Lady Marion Phillips acquired a Frenches as a good working Poodle. This dog was apparently used at Crufts by one

Int. Ch. Nunsoe Duc de la Terasse of Blakeen: A top winning Poodle in the 1930s.

UK. Am. Can. Ch. Bibelot's Tall Dark and Handsome.

of the top dog food firms to advertise their products. Also noteworthy is Mrs Proctor's fine Tzigane kennel of brown Standards.

INT. CH. NUNSOE DUC DE LA TERRASSE OF BLAKEEN

One of the most notable of Standard Poodles, said to have exerted the greatest influence on the breed was the Triple International Champion Nunsoe Duc de la Terrasse of Blakeen. This dog was Imported from Switzerland in 1932 by Jane Lane. A truly elegant dog with a great character, he is in most of the pedigrees of Standard

Poodles. He later crossed the Atlantic and was quickly campaigned to his American Title by Mrs. Sherman Hoyt after joining the Blakeen kennels. He went on to win Best in Show at the Poodle Club of America Speciality 1934 and 1936, and won Best in Show at Westiminster in 1935. Most of the early Poodles in America were imported from the British Isles.

TALL, DARK AND HANDSOME

British, American and Canadian Champion Bibelot's Tall Dark and Handsome (TDH), owned by Susan Frazer, caused

quite a sensation in England after being imported from Canada. This outstanding dog made a significant impact on British Standard Poodles and, indeed, on Standards throughout the world

A Canadian Champion at the tender age of seven months, in only five days of showing he then gained his American title at 11 months. He departed for England to be released from quarantine just three days before Crufts Dog Show 1965, where he took the Reserve Challenge Certificate. He was handled by Marilyn Willis.

Not just a pretty face, or indeed worthy specimen of the breed, TDH competed at and

Am. Can. Ch. Lemerle Travelin Lite.

won 30 British Shows, totalling 13 Best in Shows, as well as achieving highest scoring on numerous occasions in Obedience.

When he retired from showing in 1968 he had 31 Best in Shows in three countries to his credit. TDH surpassed all expectations in siring not only many beautiful Champions, but also many quality Standard Poodles that are the foundation of many of the top British lines today. His qualities live on. A truly great dog is not just one that achieves success in the show ring. His sweet and charming temperament was renown. Said

to be 'small' by some Standard Poodle enthusiasts, we have seen that prior to 1930 (before the importation of the tall white dog, Triple International Champion Nunsoe Duc de la Terrece of Blakeen), most British Standard Poodles were 19-23 inches (48-58 cm) in size, the size that is still popular on the Continent.

THE POODLE IN AMERICA

The Poodle Club of America was formed in 1896, although it was dissolved in 1898 and reformed in 1931 when it was elected to membership of the American Kennel Club (AKC).

Many Poodles were exported

from the UK to the USA during the 1980s. Later, several kennels were breeding good 'types' of Poodle, mostly the Standards, while only a few were devoted to the Miniature. Mrs Sherman Hoyt imported the Miniature Champion Algie of Piperscroft from Mrs G.L. Boyd, and Sparkling Jet. These dogs were said to have a tremendous influence on Miniature Poodles in the US. Mrs Whitehouse Walker-Carillon was an important breeder, while the Venas kennel owned by Mrs Audrey Tyndall in England, had a considerable influence in Miniature Poodles in America.

The Cartlane Kennels bred Toy Poodles. America seemed to take more interest in this size Poodle and held their own size classes before the UK. Breeders of the early small Poodles included, Mrs Evelyn Barnes, Mrs Sherman Hoyt, Mr C.K. Cobin with the Nibroc Kennel, Mrs Audrey Watts and Mrs Gladys Hertel with her Gladville Kennel.

Few Poodles were shown and registered, as the breed was far less popular in the USA than it was in England. Perseverance from American breeders, such as Miss Alger, Mr and Mrs Trevor, Mr Moulyon and Mr Jacobson firmly established the breed in the USA.

All the colours were encouraged and today classes for solid colours are scheduled at the American shows, although parti-colours can be seen at some breed club shows. Great strides were made in the breeding of the Toy Poodle. One of the best known dogs was Ch. Barnes Wee Winnie Winkle, bred by Evelyn Barnes. Poodles have been significant in winning high honours at top American shows. In 1997, Toy Poodle Ch. Smash JP Win A Victory and Standard Poodle Ch. Brighton Minimoto each won Best in Group.

CONFORMATION SHOW STARS

The quality of the Poodles shown at Crufts is of the highest standard seen anywhere. In 1950 Mr & Mrs L.H.C. Coventon's blue Miniature Poodle, Ch. Adastra Magic Beau, was awarded Supreme Best in Show at Crufts. The white Miniature owned by Paul Williams and R. Boatright, Ch. Rocksville The Cool Dude At Glynpedr, bred by J. Shaw, was runner-up to the winner of the Utility Group in 1997. This stunning dog won 47 CCs before he was retired at Crufts 1999 after taking Best of Breed.

The Crufts 1999 runner-up to the Utility Group winner was the charismatic Toy Poodle, Tuttlebees Witchcraft, owned by Angela Corish and Norman Butcher.

THE CURRENT SCENE IN THE UK

Poodles from different countries continue to have an impact on the breed in the UK. We have seen some magnificent silvers, as well as leading whites and other colours passing on their attributes to their progeny.

In the show ring we have seen significant changes as a result of new laws affecting quarantine. With the advent of the Pet Passport scheme, dogs are now able to compete in shows all over Europe and in the USA and many exhibitors are taking advantage of this to gain International titles for their dogs. Although there is a slight variation of the Breed Standard with the AKC and the FCI (Federation Cynologique Internationale) this doesn't seem to be noticeable within the breed itself, certainly not with the Poodles shown here to date.

Pet Poodles have also benefited from these relaxed quarantine rules and pet owners can now travel with their dogs on the Pet Passport scheme. In either case the dogs must travel with up to date veterinary health certificates.

New laws regarding tail docking may well have an impact on the future of the breed. Docked Poodles born after April 2007 are not permitted to be exhibited in any shows in the UK where the public pay an entrance fee.

Ch. Adastra Magic Beau: Crufts Best in Show, 1950.

Ch. Ir. Ch. Grayco Hazlenut: Crufts Best in Show 1982.

In 1955 a brown Standard Poodle owned by Mrs April Proctor, Ch. Tzigane Aggri of Nashend, won Supreme Best in Show at Crufts. In 1982, it was the turn of the one-time record holder, the brown Toy poodle, Lesley Howard's, Ch/Ir Ch Grayco Hazelnut.

1966 was the year of distinction for a delightful character in the shape of the Toy Poodle owned by Clare Coxall (formerly Perry), Ch. Oakington Puckshill Ambersunblush (Sunshine), bred by Mrs Myles Dobson. This charming little apricot achieved Supreme Best in Show.

A notable Miniature to make an impact on the breed was the black Ch. Tiopepi Typhoon, born in 1993. A well-travelled dog, he spent time in the USA, gained his title out there and

then came back through quarantine to return to his home with Clare Coxall. Typhoon was a top producer; among his children were Ch. Tiopepi Take by Storm, Ch. Tiopepi Tornado and Ch. Tiopepi Tyrant.

Never one to stop at producing top Miniature Poodles, Clare bred the Crufts 1985 Best in Show winner, the Standard Poodle Ch. Montravia Tommy Gun. Owned by Pauline and Marita Gibbs and handled by Marita (now Rogers), Tommy established the record as top-winning Standard Poodle. He won 53 CCs.

In 1967, as we have seen, the Standard Poodle, Can. Am. Ch. Bibelots Tall Dark and Handsome (Tramp), won Reserve Best in Show. His double grandsire became an influential and much noted and

loved Standard Poodle, Ch. Vicmars Balnoble Royale (Sam), owned by Vicky Marshall and bred by Anne Beswick.

'Sam' had a distinguished show career, winning many CCs. He was a Group winner and Best in Show winner. A dog of great character and noted by many top breeders as being one of the best dogs to be produced in the UK, 'Sam' was to sire many Champions as well as many great quality Standard Poodles that can be found in most of the top winning pedigrees throughout the world.

The significant black, Ch. The Detonator of Leander, was top Standard for two years with a total of 36 CCs.

In more recent years imports have made quite an impact on the show scene as well as

Eng. Am. Ned. Int. Ch. Pinafore Seabiskit (Imp) owned by Marlene Carter and Penny Harney. Winner under UK, US and FCI rules. Making his mark as a sire for silver Standards in the UK.

producing quality puppies. The white Standard Ch. Topscore Contradiction took Best in Show at Crufts in 2002, and BIS at the World Show in the same year. He is owned by Astrid Giercksky and was handled by Mikael Nilsson.

Toy Poodle Ch. Aedan Double Delight, owned by Sandra and Beryl Godfrey, won a Group at Crufts along with many other outstanding wins.

Another top winner was the Toy Breed record holder, Valerie Dunn's white, Ch. Valetta Love Affair.

We have seen the black Miniature Poodle, Ch. Minarets Secret Assignment, winning the Group at Crufts, and Best in Show at various shows. He took the Breed record number of CC wins to 64 (at the time of writing). He is owned and handled by Melanie Harwood.

The only UK-bred to win the Poodle Club of America national specialty in recent years was Standard Poodle Ch. Afterglow The Big Tease, co-owned by Michael Gadsby and Michael Pawasarat at the time. He has also won Best in Show in England and was top dog in 2008.

TOP WINNERS:
STANDARD, MINIATURE AND TOY

Ch. Am. Ch. Afterglow The Big Tease, bred by Mike Gadsby and owned by Jason Lynn. This stunning Standard Poodle has won on both sides of the Atlantic.

Photo courtesy of Les Denman.

Ch. Minarets Secret Assignment: The all-time top CC winner for Miniature Poodles, owned by Melanie Harwood.

Ch. Valetta Love Affair: Toy breed recordholder.

A POODLE FOR YOUR LIFESTYLE

Chapter 3

There is no mystery about why the Poodle attracts such large numbers of prospective owners. This striking, intelligent and affectionate breed has a lot to offer the right owner. However, anyone considering taking on a dog needs to consider the huge commitment involved and to take a long, hard look at their lifestyle to see whether dog ownership is appropriate.

COMMITMENT

Before purchasing a Poodle it is a good idea to understand the breed, why it was bred, for what use, and to be aware of certain inherited behavioural traits. You will also need to decide on which size of Poodle is right for you, how much time you are able to devote to your dog each day, whether you want a male or female, show dog or pet. Further considerations include any other pets you may have, whether you have children, and the level of training you need and want to do with your Poodle. It is very important to consider all these factors carefully, to ensure you choose the right dog for you and your family. You will, after all have your Poodle for at least 12-14 years.

It is a big commitment to take on a lively breed that needs physical exercise and mental stimulation.

This is a breed that thrives on human companionship.

EXERCISE AND STIMULATION

All dogs need to walk. All dog owners should acquire the habit of walking the dog. Fish need to swim, birds need to fly, and dogs need to walk. Your Poodle will need to be walked on a daily basis for at least 30 minutes. Twice a day is better. Walking is important for their mind and body.

Those who buy a Poodle and then leave it at home all day while they go out to work and want to know why their dog is chewing everything in sight, obviously do not understand the importance of inheritance. If you want a slow, lazy breed, don't buy a Poodle. The Poodle is an active dog with great intelligence. And while he is kind, gentle and sweet, he is not a dog designed to be a couch potato in his youth. The Poodle has an active, bright, quick-thinking mind, and will hold his own with other working and retriever breeds because of his ancestral lineage. I will not dispute that some Poodles (of all sizes) have developed a more addled brain and will be perfectly content to become the pom-pom adorned layabout, especially later in life. With owners to match, a compatible life is ensured. But those who aspire to own a tranquil companion may find themselves with a Poodle who has inherited from its ancestors a strong sense to work. If you want a Poodle, you must be prepared to give him plenty of mental and physical stimulation.

COMPANIONSHIP

The Poodle is a people dog. It is a very tactile breed. The Poodle loves to be touching his owner – lying against his owner's legs, lying with his head on his owner's feet, etc. – and he loves his owner touching him, which is an asset in training. The Poodle craves human companionship and is never happier than when he is with his owner. A Poodle will follow his owner all over the house – upstairs to the bathroom, back down again, from one room to the next, up and down the garden with the lawn mower; where you settle, he lies down to sleep. A Poodle will prefer to ride in the car with you rather than be left at home on his own. But a trained Poodle will happily stay when told and wait to be called or for you to return.

Weigh up the costs involved in Poodle ownership before taking the plunge.

The Poodle is a very good mind reader. He knows when your mood is active or when you are feeling low and he will respond likewise. He knows when you put your 'walking' clothes on and will let you know by dancing around your feet, sometimes unable to contain squeaks of delight at the thought of going out for a run. He also knows, and hates it, when you are cross or upset for whatever reason. He will either pester you with constant nudges with his nose or curl up and sigh, throwing worried glances at you from time to time. If he thinks you are displeased with him for unfair reasons, he will sulk.

Not a guarding breed by nature, the Poodle is nonetheless very protective and will sense very quickly when his owner is not keen on somebody. He will make plenty of noise when strangers approach. Some callers ask me, "How can you stand all that noise?" I smile because the Poodle is simply telling the

stranger to "mind your manners or else!" Once the caller is spoken to as a friend and invited in, the Poodle will accept the friend, provided the attitude of the person is such that the Poodle feels comfortable and senses his owner is happy. The Poodle is not a dog that will bite unless he is put under extreme provocation, badly reared, or has a serious health problem. And then it is more of a nip than a bite, in most cases. Poodles have been trained for centuries to protect by fanciers, individuals, and some police organisations. For a long time the Poodle has served as such an excellent companion to families or individuals who require the most loyal friend possible.

FINANCES

It is a good idea to establish the cost of purchasing and keeping

this breed by asking around and talking to breeders. The price of a puppy will vary slightly from breeder to breeder and from dog to dog (e.g. a show-quality dog may cost a little more than a pet), but the purchase price is only the start of your financial commitment to dog ownership.

Feeding can prove expensive for any breed of dog. If you plan to feed commercially prepared dog food, it is worth bearing in mind that you get what you pay for. If you plan to feed a home-cooked diet, you will find that the Poodle is not a fussy eater, and expensive cuts of meat are not necessary. He will happily eat tripe and other reasonably priced raw meat, along with vegetables and cereals, and does very well on it.

Other ongoing costs include the price of pet insurance, routine worming and parasite

Generally Poodles will live in harmony with other dogs, regardless of size.

pampered Miniature stay with me for a month. After one day of sulking, this small indulged, silk-bedroom, satin-covered, lounge-living lap dog, took off when we were out walking over the rough terrain of marsh area near my home and chased and caught a rabbit.

Most Poodles are insanely enthusiastic about chasing birds. Without any training at all a Poodle will chase a bird across the garden, a field, or along the beach, for what sometimes may appear to be miles; until he either catches it and immediately returns it to his owner (as his retrieving instinct demands) or the bird flies so high that the Poodle accepts it is beyond his grasp, so he gives up – until the next bird comes along. Some Poodles will quite naturally point a bird, get it up and then leap into the air to catch it. Mine have done this with pheasants. They do not harm the bird and I set it free.

Poodles that are not properly introduced to other pets or to livestock may get into the habit of chasing other animals, or indeed, anything that moves. This instinct has to be channelled and controlled. Dogs have been killed when chasing cars, and animals have been killed from fright or from a few dogs worked into a frenzy of excitement. It is vital that you appreciate the amount of time you will have to spend on socialising and training your Poodle (see Chapter Six), not only in the first few months of ownership, but throughout the rest of his life.

control, all of which add up. In addition to this, it is essential to find out about the cost of clipping before taking on this breed (see below).

POODLES AND OTHER PETS
The Poodle is sweet, companionable and very sociable with other people and dogs. Cats and other dogs in the household, can be gradually introduced and will usually live alongside one another very well. Rabbits can be more of a problem, as they seem to bring out the chase instinct in a Poodle. The Poodle behavioural inheritance does affect the way in which he is able to live alongside animals. Often a Poodle will chase a wild rabbit or hare and if he catches it he will kill it on contact. I once had a very

POODLES AND CHILDREN

As with all pets, the earlier in life that a Poodle puppy can be introduced to children, the better. The dam of the litter is normally very protective of her puppies until they are about four weeks old, then it becomes relatively easy to introduce new things into the puppies' lives. Children can be asked to sit on the floor and the puppies can take their time in exploring and playing with them. I have not had a problem with children of any age visiting my Poodles or viewing puppies from the age of six weeks. This is because I take charge of the situation. I like children to visit the pups as it is great socialisation that will hold them in good stead for the future.

When deciding on a puppy for a family I tend to draw the attention to certain elements of a puppy that I feel will be most suitable for the lifestyle of each particular family. So far, this has worked out very well.

GROOMING

The Poodle coat is unique and will grow endlessly. If never brushed it will either felt like a sheep, or the coat will grow into spirals that, if left untrimmed, would grow to the ground. If you intend to take on a Poodle, you will need to make ongoing arrangements to care for this amazing coat. There are different types of trim, which vary according to the dog's role (see Chapter Five). Through the generations fashion has altered these trims, exaggerating them even. But trimming for Poodles has been in existence for centuries. It is no new and modern trend.

Most people enjoy their Poodles looking smart and well trimmed. Some owners learn to trim the coat themselves, while others may use a professional groomer. Constant visits to the grooming parlour cost money. The Poodle owner must be made aware of this outlay, or they must be prepared to learn the art of trimming themselves. The Poodle's coat must not be left to its own devices; it must have regular attention for the health of the dog. The coat must be trimmed on a regular basis, every six weeks, to prevent thick mats or felts forming. The hair must be brushed and combed daily, or at least three to four times a week. It is, therefore, an important consideration before purchasing a Poodle to think about coat care, and to check out the cost of grooming. Of course, you can

Children and Poodles are a great mix, as long as interactions are carefully supervised.

To begin with there is not much work involved in looking after a Poodle coat.

The workload steps up dramatically if you decide to keep your Poodle in show trim.

learn to do this yourself, if you have the aptitude, and somebody kind enough to teach you, but not everybody wants to clip their own dog. So how much will it cost every 4-6 weeks to visit a professional groomer? Do ring round and find out, so that you can incorporate this cost into the rearing. There is a relatively standard price amongst groomers, but the trim and amount of hair required to be groomed and bathed will make a significant difference to price. Time and effort has to be paid for. A groomer could spend one hour on a Toy Poodle and four hours or more on a Poodle in show trim, or the larger Poodle whose

coat is in poor condition, matted etc.

The appearance of the Poodle is important. The Poodle loves to feel he looks good. Whichever haircut you decide upon for your Poodle, it should compliment his graceful carriage and show off his wonderful face and expressive eyes. A Poodle with a clipped face shows a wide spectrum of emotions, from laughter to tears. The Poodle can look happy, sad, sardonic, sympathetic, critical and complimentary. Trims chosen for the Poodle must suit his purpose and allow for flexible, free movement to perform his chosen activity.

Coat changes when the Poodle

loses his easy-to-manage puppy hair sometimes cause the inexperienced owner problems. The loose wool can felt close to the skin and the unsuspecting owner, regularly brushing without parting the coat and getting the comb down to the skin to remove the dead hair, will get quite a shock to find the professional groomer has to shave the dog to the skin in order to remove the felt.

As a rule, puppies have their feet and face and the base of their tail clipped from four to five weeks of age, every week by the breeder, to get them used to the procedure. Then the pet dog needs to be clipped every four weeks or so by the new owner or professional groomer, and the show dog every week. The body hair is not usually clipped while the puppy is under four or five months, but it is shaped with scissors. We will look at the different styles in Chapter Five, but as a rule, the adult Poodle will have a trim to suit the dog and owner's way of life. For example, if the dog is working, or constantly running on the beach, the Sporting trim may be the best trim all round. The Lamb trim leaves trousers on the legs and is relatively easy to manage for the average pet owner. These trims are the most popular in the average grooming salon.

Puppies are highly impressionable so the golden rule is to start as you mean to go on.

POSITIVE PUPPYHOOD

Before considering taking on a Poodle, it is vital to understand the pitfalls that can occur if the owner makes mistakes rearing the puppy. Many mistakes can be made completely unintentionally. Unfortunately, some owners teach their pups early bad habits by teasing them, or carrying the smaller varieties around like babies. It's a good idea to remember that size is in our heads, not the dog's. All Poodles, regardless of size, think they are dogs. People, without thinking, chase puppies. Rough handling, such as patting heavily, boxing (whether you touch or not) particularly around the face, can cause or encourage an aggressive or protective reaction. This may cause squeals of delight in the

unsuspecting owner (particularly a child) but these silly games are a form of teaching excitability and may set a less passive dog on the road to hostility. Luckily, the Poodle is basically a very good-natured dog and tolerates, or copes quite well with, wayward, untrained owners.

Poodles of all sizes love to retrieve. They will retrieve practically anything without much encouragement from us. Articles such as a ball, a stick, slippers, socks, stockings ... in fact, anything that happens to be at a puppy's nose level will be investigated by his mouth, picked up where possible and carried. All puppies use their mouths to investigate. Tiny puppies have sharp, needle-like teeth, so if the item of exploration happens to be your leg or a child's arm

discomfort will result. If you cry out in pain when the excitable pups bites it will immediately drop its prey. A substitute such as its own toy, or a raw bone to chew can then be given. Give them safe toys to chew such as indestructible Kongs stuffed with some favourite food, and raw bones to gnaw to exercise their mouth and relieve the pain of teething. Yes, even Toy Poodles love to chew on a raw bone or chicken wing.

As a youngster the Poodle will need to be kept busy or he will develop bad, or undesirable habits and ways of keeping himself amused. Digging up carpet, chewing furniture – all sorts of disturbing behaviour will result when such an active, intelligent dog is left to his own devices for hour upon hour, every day.

Once you have a Poodle (of any age, but particularly a puppy), you will need to devote a certain amount of time each day to the rudiments of training – Stand, Sit, Down, Come, Stay, Fetch, etc. Your Poodle should also be meeting other people, children, dogs, cats, and other animals as often as possible. (See Chapter Six for more information about training and socialisation.) Unless you are prepared to incorporate this into your daily routine, do not get a Poodle (or any dog).

The Poodle is a glamorous breed, but these dogs are also highly intelligent and need the chance to use their brains.

It is a great bonus if you can take your Poodle on holiday.

The sex you choose is a matter of personal preference.

HOLIDAYS

The Poodle makes a great travelling companion. He is generally excellent in the car and enjoys caravanning with his owner. This is a great way to holiday. But for those who spend time travelling abroad, and do not want to take their beloved pet with them, it is essential to consider what will happen to your Poodle in your absence.

There are many excellent 'dog nannies' available. Some advertise locally, in vet surgeries, for example, while others advertise nationally in the canine press and on Poodle websites. It is wonderful if you can find a house/pet sitter to live-in while you are away, or a trusted friend to take care of your pet. The Poodle doesn't always fare well in kennels when he has been used to living in a comfortable home, but if this is essential, then it is best to check out any recommended kennel for comfort, care and cost.

NARROWING THE SEARCH

If you have taken a long, hard look at your life and have decided that you can make the necessary adjustments to give a Poodle the home this magnificent dog truly deserves, the next consideration is to think about the type of Poodle that you want.

WHICH VARIETY?

All sizes of Poodle make great pets, but your family and home may be more suited to one particular size. People living in flats with no immediate access to a garden should not have a dog at all. However, Poodles of all sizes can live quite happily in a large or small house. All sizes should be adequately exercised.

Choosing the size of the Poodle you want comes down to personal preference. Some people love small dogs; others prefer large dogs. Consider whether it is better to have a Toy Poodle around your children, as a Standard Poodle could knock over small children during play. Regardless of size, adequate socialisation and training is essential.

MALE OR FEMALE?

There is little difference between the male and female temperament. However, if you choose a bitch, you must be prepared for her coming into season. The female may start her menstrual cycle at any time from 8 to 16 months. Both sexes should have a sweet disposition and be easy to train, although

POODLE COLOURS

White.

Black.

Red.

males sometimes take a bit longer to mature.

Both sexes can show dominance by mounting other dogs. Puppies tend to do this, but grow out of it. Castration and spaying (neutering), is often done far too early in my opinion. If this procedure is necessary I firmly believe the Poodle should have the time to mature (i.e. be at least one year old – later for the Standard Poodle) before the operation is undertaken.

Very often when males and females are kept together, it is the female who is alpha (top) dog, rather than the male. The most difficult time when keeping both sexes is when the female comes

into season. Even a castrated dog can become aroused and mate the bitch, the only difference being that no pups will result.

COLOUR

Originally the Poodle came in solid colours and parti-colour. The solid colour has been preferred for at least the last 50 years, perfected by breeders. The parti-colour (two, and more rarely, three-coloured) Poodle was virtually bred out, as it was not advisable to mix parti with solids and dilute good colours. Although the parti does have supporters, the Breed Standard requires solid colours (though some, including the blue and the

silver, may take time to clear). These include black, blue, silver, white, cream, apricot and brown. The mixing of colours must be seriously studied or mis-marks may result.

In all colours there may be a slight variation in the texture of the coat, some being easier to groom, some being curlier than others and the crisp coat more pronounced in some.

You may have a preference for colour. Apart from the black and the white, the colour in Poodles varies in shade, especially on the ears. The black can fade in later years. The brown, blue, silver and apricot can come in lighter or darker shades. Then there is

Apricot.   Blue.   Silver.

cream – which may stay cream or lighten to white. The blue and silver may take up to two years, or more, to fully clear, but at eight weeks of age their colour is defined on the face. Typically, silver will have a bright silver face and a charcoal coat at eight weeks (at four/five weeks when the breeder first clips the face evidence of this is seen). Sometimes the body coat is mistaken for black, but if you put a black and silver together you will see the distinct difference. Blues may be a bit harder to define, but I like my blues to have a distinct true silver/blue muzzle and blue cheeks at eight weeks.

Browns can come in dark red-brown to the coffee and cream of café-au-lait. Again, the face at eight weeks of age gives a good indication of what the colour will clear to, though this is not set in stone. Colours are often mixed when breeding, and there is nothing wrong with this – up to a point. To retain good pigment as required by the Breed Standard, one would not consider mating brown to white – or waste a good silver by incorporating brown in the pedigree. Brown can be mated to black, but better not when the black has a white parent. The same care must be taken when breeding apricot. If you are fussy

about colour, check the pedigree. If you want to show your Poodle then it may pay to be fussy.

Pigmentation is extremely important on the show dog. The brown will have a brown nose, lips, pads, eye rims, and should have dark amber eyes. In the other colours black points are desirable, and essential if you want to win in the show ring with a white or cream. Dark skin is preferable to pink skin in the show dog and is considered to be tougher. The eyes should be a very dark brown, almost black in appearance. Light eyes should be taken at face value with other faults, such as a narrow rib cage or heavy head.

45

POODLE COLOURS

Brown.

Café au Lait.

Cream.

PET, SHOW OR WORKING DOG?

If you have specific plans for your Poodle – whether you want a pet and companion, a dog to compete in the show ring, a dog to work with, or a Poodle that will compete in Agility or Obedience – it is a good idea to try to find a Poodle with the right temperament and physical conformation for the task at hand. For example, if you intend to show your dog, you will need to purchase a puppy that has show-ring potential. A pet puppy may have a few minor conformation faults that would in no way detract from his ability to make a fantastic companion or working dog, but would curtail his success in the show ring. Before purchasing your Poodle, enquire whether his ancestors were energetic, sports-orientated fun dogs, or serene and laid back with no keen notion to participate in exciting activity. Of course, this will not 'guarantee' that your puppy will develop likewise, but it will go a long way in giving you an idea of your Poodle's future temperament.

To an owner who despairs of the tricks his Poodle gets up to, (interpreted as naughty) I can only say, take courage; you have yourself a Poodle of the lineage of great intelligence.

Poodles love to be active, they

It is important to decide what ambitions you have for your Poodle before you choose a puppy.

like to show off, they like to socialise, so they will invariably love going to dog shows. If you intend to show your Poodle and you have no experience, then attend local ring-training classes, go to some local shows to see what happens, talk to your breeder to discuss the good – and not so good – parts of your dog's construction. Be realistic, and above all, have as much fun as your Poodle will. Many a pet dog has been sold to a pet owner who then decides to take up showing. If you want to purchase a show dog and you have no experience, it may be advisable to take along somebody who knows a bit about the breed. But trust in your breeder will go a long way in establishing success.

CHOOSING A POODLE

Having checked that your lifestyle is appropriate for a dog and having decided on what kind of Poodle you want, how do you go about finding the right dog?

FINDING A BREEDER

With the internet it is now possible to find litters of puppies listed for sale through Poodle clubs. Other than this the dog papers and local newspapers sometimes have advertisements for puppies. Also, any breed club or the Kennel Club can be contacted to find breeders. Please do your homework to ensure that you find a reputable breeder who genuinely cares about their dogs.

Most breeders do care passionately. They breed and rear to the best of their abilities, testing for inherited diseases and finding suitable stud dogs that are not too closely related. However, there are some disreputable breeders out there, as well as puppy farmers, who don't care for the pup's welfare or yours, as long as they make money. Avoid these at all costs. Too many people have bought a puppy from these unscrupulous breeders only to experience heartbreak and significant financial costs.

Be sure to ask questions about the rearing and parentage of your potential puppy. If you are

You need to find a breeder with a reputation for producing Poodles that are sound in mind and body and that are typical of the breed.

unsure, walk away. It may be advisable to consult a Poodle breed club or try to locate other owners who have purchased a puppy from the same source.

Generally breeders stick with one, or two colours. So if you have decided upon a colour of your choice, if you are specific, your breed club will direct you to the breeders involved with that colour. Some people do have a hard and fast rule about the colour of the Poodle they want, others really don't mind. Often, when visiting a breeder and seeing a litter, people will change their minds. That white pup that they said they would never want

to own suddenly becomes irresistible.

Ask the breeder in the initial telephone call how they rear their puppies – house or kennel. Puppies reared in a home environment may have experienced better socialisation, although the dedicated breeder will be able to ensure that even kennel-reared puppies receive adequate socialisation. Be specific and ask questions about whether the puppies are familiar with other animals, the sound of the washing machine, etc.

Ask your breeder about their views on vaccination and feeding for good health, to see if they are

compatible with your own. Also ask what health checks they have carried out, especially if you are looking to buy a Poodle from the smaller variety where eye status will need to be known. Breeders of the Standard Poodle do not have the same level of worry with eye conditions that the smaller sizes have. Steer clear of breeders of these varieties who don't undertake eye testing (see Chapter 8 for more details about eye problems in the Poodle).

Check when the bitch last had a litter and ask about the pedigree, Kennel Club registration and any endorsements in place.

Find out as much as you can about the litter before you go to visit the breeder.

Some of the puppies may already be booked as a reputable breeder often has a waiting list.

Endorsements are put in place to protect the pup as far as possible into his future. Some of these restrictions include: not to be bred from without breeder's consent, not to change homes without breeder's knowledge, not to be exported. A good breeder will always be at the other end of the telephone to help you if required.

Be aware that most popular or well-known breeders of good reputation have a waiting list for puppies. It is a good idea to visit your chosen breeder, be introduced to their Poodles, and book a puppy from a forthcoming litter. Otherwise,

you will take pot luck as to what is available at the time, if indeed there are any puppies not already booked.

CHOOSING A PUPPY

Often, the puppy will choose you! However, the breeder knows their litter, or should do, as individuals. They will see as they begin weaning at around 4-5 weeks how characters are developing and the make and shape of a good puppy. If you want a show dog, the breeder of experience will be able to pick the right pup – barring unforeseen circumstances like missing teeth – and can

generally pick the right pup for you. Quality breeders breed quality pups. It is quite normal for more than one or two pups of a litter to be quite outstanding, with the suitable temperament to become a show dog. With the Miniature and Toy Poodle, his growth may prove a problem if it were to grow oversize for the variety. But where the breeder is established with their line, they very often know which puppies are suitable for the show ring. That's not to say that the remainder are not good puppies, and something like a lighter eye than desired for the show ring will not bother a pet owner. So

CHOOSING A PUPPY

The puppies should be kept in a clean, hygienic environment and appear lively and out-going.

The breeder will help you to assess show potential.

again, a certain amount of trust in the breeder is required, unless you have the good luck to have a good-eye for the right dog.

However, you may take a liking to a certain pup and the breeder may be willing to reserve that one for you. If possible visit the litter at least twice to get to know them. Also the pups will remember your scent and feel easier when they leave with you to go to their new home. Assuming you have done your homework on the breeder and you are happy about the way the litter has been reared and their friendliness, you shouldn't go too far wrong. If you don't trust the breeder then you shouldn't continue with the purchase.

Generally, Poodles are not shy. When you visit the litter the puppies will more than likely jump all over you and provide many licks. They will, however, sleep heavily and ignore you when very tired, or may shiver when you pick them up, so don't mistake this for being shy.

The puppies should look and smell good. If they have runny tummies avoid them. The feeding may be incorrect, or they may have an infection. They should be clean and well covered and not thin with weak bones from poor feeding. They will play around you and entertain you.

Puppies normally leave the breeder from about eight weeks of age. This is a good time for the pup to move and become part of the new family. At this age the puppy will quickly settle into a new routine and make friends with other dogs and the children in the household. Steer clear of any breeder who will allow you to take a puppy before this age.

HEALTH CHECKS
Different health checks are required for the three sizes. As a rule, for instance, the larger Poodle does not suffer the same inherent eye problems as the smaller varieties. On the other hand the Standard Poodle can inherit a skin condition called Sebaceous Adenitis, which is seen less in the smaller Poodles. All conscientious breeders will have undertaken health checks on their stock. Nobody in his right mind would want to sell a puppy that is not healthy in any way. Being a breed that suffers little with hip problems, many breeders will not risk an anaesthetic to have hips scored.

THE NEW ARRIVAL

Chapter 4

Before you bring your new puppy home, you will need to 'puppy-proof' your home environment to ensure that it is safe for the latest addition to your family and that nothing important to you is likely to be destroyed during a puppy's inevitable 'explorations'.

IN THE GARDEN

Your garden needs to be fully secured for any dog, not least a pup. Fences must be of a type the pup cannot get through. Plants that may be precious need to be put out of reach, or fenced round. Plants hazardous to animals must be removed. Your gardening book or the local nursery will be able to help you identify poisonous plants and flowers. There are lots of plants and herbs that are perfectly safe for puppies – even very good for them – keeping worms at bay as well as supplying valuable nutrients. Check these out and plant accordingly.

Poodles like to dig, and eat soil. This is perfectly okay as long as you don't mind filling in the holes. They do get certain nutrients from earth, though chemically fertilised ground could be dangerous. Puppies can demolish a piece of flowered garden, but never fear, they usually grow out of this and the garden will bounce back the next

Puppies love to explore, so make sure your garden is safe and secure.

While you are waiting for your puppy to arrive, you can buy all the equipment you will need.

surprising what you can find at this level.

It's a good idea to decide on a place to put the pup's daytime bed, or a safe area for when you are not watching him.

BUYING EQUIPMENT

The major items required for the new arrival are a brush, comb, bed, den (material), feeding and water bowls, collar and lead, toys and chews. The pet or show puppy will need daily attention to his coat, so grooming equipment will be needed, too,

GROOMING EQUIPMENT

Even if you intend to use the services of a professional groomer, you will need to groom your Poodle on a daily basis, and will therefore need a slicker brush and a wide-tooth metal comb. These are available from virtually any pet shop, and many garden centres now have a pet sales area. If you are planning to trim your Poodle yourself, you will need more equipment (see Chapter Five).

BED AND BEDDING

The bed can be a piece of veterinary bedding or fleece blanket, which is easily washable and dries in minutes in the tumble drier. You may like to purchase a comfy bed, but do make sure the pup has room to grow into the bed, or you will be buying another as he grows, especially if he is a large Poodle. Some puppies like a den. There are now material dens on sale, and many dogs find these more acceptable than a metal crate.

year. However, they may continue to dig certain areas where they find certain nutrients.

IN THE HOUSE

You will have decided beforehand where the puppy is to sleep, and which areas of the house may be out of bounds to a tiny puppy. However, it takes a tough owner to ignore the cry of a young, lonely puppy. Wherever you or the children are is where your puppy will want to be, and why not, seeing that he is, to me, a family member.

Baby gates make good temporary barriers for the pup likely to get up to mischief when you have to go out and leave him for a while, to protect him from hurting himself. Remember to make sure that television and other electrical wires or cables are safely tucked away and that cleaners and bleaches, which could prove fatal, are safely out of reach. One way to help make sure you have everything covered is to get down on your hands and knees and look at your home from a puppy's perspective. It's

CRATE/CAGE

Cages are useful as a safe haven for limited periods, or for overnight training when the dog is sleeping in your bedroom, although my pups sleep on a duvet beside our bed from as early as eight weeks and never wet. Once the lights are out they sleep until activity stirs them.

BOWLS

Your puppy will need fresh, clean water left down at all times. For this the earthenware dog bowls are excellent. They are not easy to tip over. For his food he can have the same type of bowl, or a stainless steel one. Both are easy to clean.

COLLAR AND LEAD

For a puppy, nylon collars and leads are excellent. They are relatively inexpensive so a new larger one can be purchased when the pup grows out of the collar. Do be sure the fastener is secure. Fit the collar not too tightly, but tight enough so that the puppy doesn't pull his head through it when he backs away or leaps about.

The lead needs to be average length, not short, or extended. The puppy will learn to walk at your side on a loose lead, and not walk miles ahead, or tug you.

For the older dog, or larger Poodle, a rolled leather collar may be better. Many exhibitors use thin, rolled collars to show their dogs as it does not mark the coat.

Fleecy veterinary bedding is machine washable and easy to dry.

TOYS AND CHEWS

Do not be tempted to buy cheap rubber toys with a squeaky inside. Your pup will chew them in no time and could swallow the bits, to his detriment. 'Kongs' are indestructible toys that can be stuffed with food and will keep a puppy occupied for some time, giving teething exercise. Raw, meaty bones are excellent - perfect for puppies to chew from the age of eight weeks. I use rib bones, and puppies have one to chew after exercise and food. They also love to chew on a cabbage leaf or piece of broccoli, or a carrot.

Do not give your puppy old shoes to chew. He will not know the difference between old and new, so he can't be blamed for then chewing any shoe. Instead, purchase puppy toys fit for the purpose, such as ropes and knotted toys, hard rubber balls and indestructible nylon or rubber bones.

ID

You may also like to think about identification of your puppy.

The toys you buy must be tough enough to withstand chewing.

Many breeders now microchip their puppies, and will give the new owner the papers supporting this. Some tattoo the ear. Some people prefer just to put an identification tag on the dog's collar. You may like to talk this over with your breeder and vet.

FINDING A VET

Every dog should be registered with a good vet. Finding one is usually best done by recommendation. Talking to people with dogs will bring forth much information about vets. Give them a ring, or pop into the surgery to find out about times and procedures. Introduce yourself to the vet and see if you think you will get along with him. You must be able to talk to your vet and not feel intimidated.

COLLECTING YOUR PUPPY

Your breeder will have clipped your puppy's face and feet and given him a bath, so he will look and smell gorgeous.

Be sure to take some old towels for your journey home, just in case your puppy is sick in the car. Puppies usually travel best on the back seat of the car with a passenger – human or kind dog. The presence of an older dog used to travelling will do much to put your puppy at ease and make his journey far less stressful. Alternatively, put a meaty bone on a towel on the seat for him to chew, or some toys to play with. After a while he will more than likely fall asleep.

Hopefully your puppy will have had his course of nosodes before coming to you. Nosodes are a homoeopathic alternative to conventional vaccination. In my opinion, nosodes are just as effective as conventional vaccination and have no potentially damaging side-effects. Many vets do not accept that nosodes work, but an increasing number of vets are starting to include complementary therapies, including homoeopathic remedies, in their treatment options. There is a lot of reading material available if this option interests you and the Alternative Veterinary Medicine Centre (see appendix) may be able to help you to find a vet who offers homoeopathic treatment.

If your pup has not had a course of nosodes, you can start him on day one of coming home. Even if you are persuaded to go the conventional route, the undesirable side-effects that sometimes follow conventional vaccination can, in some measure, be offset using homoeopathy. I have used this method with a puppy that was very ill following a conventional vaccine with great success.

The breeder will give you the pup's pedigree and registration, its record of worming, nosodes or vaccine record, if any, and most importantly a diet sheet, which it

If you take your puppy out at regular intervals, he will soon get the idea of house training.

but not nearly so understanding if the puppy misbehaves through sheer tiredness.

HOUSE TRAINING

Poodle puppies, especially the Standard Poodle, are very easy to house train and if you follow the procedure on taking the puppy into the garden often, as we discussed earlier, he will be house trained in a few days. Shouting at your puppy for making a mistake will set back training considerably. Rubbing your puppy's nose in the mess is *not* acceptable behaviour. Would you do that to a child?

Make sure you take the puppy into the garden first thing when he wakes in the morning, not

waiting until you have showered. Then it will be too late. Puppies, like babies, cannot hold on – they do not have the developed muscles. So minimise the opportunities for accidents by being aware and persistent with taking the pup into the garden and asking for a wee, then praising as soon as he squats.

Think about playtime. The pup is active so will need to relieve himself more. After a drink, after food, last thing at night, first thing in the morning, if you have been out and left him for a while he will need a wee immediately. Follow the simple rules and you will be amazed what a clever, clean puppy you have.

CRATE TRAINING

The use of crates for restricting the movement of puppies and older dogs is a relatively modern idea. Some trainers believe in them. I have never crated a puppy. However, it is essential, if you intend to use a crate for any reason, that you know how to acclimatise your puppy to it.

The first stage is the put the crate up. Then put bedding inside – with the puppy watching. Next put some tasty food in the crate and leave the pup to go in and get it. Do this a few times, adding a few toys as you go along, and the puppy will begin to associate the crate with good things. Do not close

It does not take long for a puppy to value his crate as his own special den.

the door at this stage. When the pup goes in the cage of his own accord – to chew a bone for example – push the door shut without making a fuss, leave it for a minute and then open it again. Do this a few times each day, building up the length of time the pup is shut in the crate to one minute. In a week or so this can be increased to five minutes, then half an hour.

Crates are *not* for your dog to live in. If you want a caged animal, you may as well get a bird or a stuffed toy dog. Some people shut their Poodles in crates at night, but I have never found that necessary with my Standard Poodles. In forty years of living with Poodles, I have never found it necessary to shut a Poodle in a cage while I go out. Having a crate for a den is another matter.

HOUSE RULES

In the wild a dog would never sleep alone, without its family and the alpha dog – pack leader. Any puppy we keep from a litter will sleep in the bedroom with us. The dogs have always had the run of the house and generally sleep either beside the bed on a duvet or in the next bedroom on the spare bed, as they like. If we have children staying they usually decide to sleep on the floor beside them.

You may not want your Poodle in the bedroom, although I can't think why. But if this is the case, then it is essential to acclimatise the pup to the place you have decided he will sleep, whether it is a bed in the kitchen or wherever you choose. You will have purchased a bed, or duvet, or fleece for your puppy. If you have another dog that sleeps in

the kitchen, your small pup may be better penned until you know you have bonded the two together.

After making sure your puppy has relieved himself, put him on or in his sleeping area with a biscuit, bone or toy, tell him to 'Stay' and walk away. The first night your puppy will probably be very tired after his eventful day, so will probably go straight to sleep. If he does not have company in the room he will more than likely wake up after a few hours of sleep and cry, as he will feel frightened and alone. It always amazes me that people wouldn't dream of letting a baby cry himself to sleep, yet they expect that of an eight-week-old puppy.

If you want your dog to become accustomed to being alone (either at night or during the day when you go out), you need to make sure he is well exercised – a pleasantly tired dog is far less likely to become worked up than a bored dog with lots of pent-up energy. Settle your dog, without making a fuss, and then quietly leave the room. You can leave him with a good-sized bone. Do not sit and cuddle the pup until he begins to worry. Treat leaving as an everyday, natural occurrence, even if it is not. Initially, leave for a very short time. On your return, do not reward your Poodle if he is overexcited. Wait until he is calm and them talk to him and give him a treat. Once your dog has accepted this, you can build up to longer periods.

Other house rules can be quickly learned. Dogs don't automatically climb on the sofa. It usually happens because people pick puppies up and cuddle them while they are sitting on the sofa and then get a shock when the puppy thinks this is where they thought their owner wanted them to be, so get on of their own accord. Indirectly, you will teach your dog by your own actions. It doesn't bother us that the dogs lie on the sofa. But, if it bothers you, then don't encourage it. Lay or sit on the floor with the pup if you fancy a cuddle and you don't want him to learn about sitting on the sofa. If the pup tries to climb on your lap while you are sitting on the sofa stand up and walk away, without saying a word. Then sit on the floor and play/cuddle the pup. He will very quickly learn that if you are sitting on the sofa you are not approachable, but if he sits on the floor you will praise him with some attention.

Follow this with any house rules you want the dog to learn. It just takes a bit of thought, and some realisation on your part of what you are actually saying to the pup by your actions, not just words (which are meaningless to an eight week old pup). Animals don't use words; they react to actions – body language.

FEEDING AND EXERCISE

Your breeder will give you a diet sheet for your new puppy. It is strongly advisable to keep to this diet, at least for a couple of

Decide on the house rules from an early stage, or your Poodle will take the law into his own hands.

weeks until the pup has settled in. Being a firm believer that dogs should be fed as closely as possible to what is natural for them, I choose to feed a raw diet of meat, vegetables, bones and a minimum of cereals, such as millet and quinoa, milk, manuka honey, tree bark powder, ground almonds and eggs.

This is a relatively economic way of feeding. Dogs do not require expensive cuts of meat or processed dog food that costs the earth. Many Poodles have intolerance to gluten, so it is wise to consider this within your feeding programme. Cottage cheese and fish, such as sardines and tuna are included in the diet, along with garlic. Nutrition is covered in the next chapter in more detail.

All dogs need exercise, but with restraint, or consideration

for growth rate. Poodles of all sizes can suffer joint damage or lameness when formal exercise is maintained for long periods at a young age. They can play for hours with far less stress to their growth and structure than going on a five mile hike every day while they are growing. However, it is important to get your puppy out to meet people and other dogs. And it is important to handle them daily and walk them sensibly.

Exercise may consist of a run in the garden or park with other dogs, or a short daily walk to heel, with a few commands – Sit, Down, Stand, Wait, followed by praise. Do not over-exercise a young puppy. Let him sleep when he wants to. When he is tired it is a good time for you to leave the pup with a raw bone and go shopping.

A puppy has to learn his place in the family pack.

EARLY LESSONS

Poodles make wonderful companions, and even more so when they are properly trained and socialised. Despite a puppy's immaturity, there is a lot you can do to begin the process of training and socialisation.

UNDERSTANDING THE PACK

The Poodle is gregarious. He is a pack animal, as are all dogs. He thrives on togetherness. It is therefore perfectly okay for the pack leader to have his pack – family – with him overnight. A Poodle will, in a matter of moments, get the message about where he will sleep as defined by the pack leader. It is not natural and takes some conditioning to get the pup to sleep alone, shut away from the family. No pack leader in the wild would do this to an eight week old puppy. They rely on each other for protection and comfort.

This is what happens in punishment. The pack leader will walk away and ignore unwanted behaviour, leaving the pup to figure out that it's better to do as the pack leader wants rather than be left alone. If you understand this about dogs, you will know why your pup cries bitterly for you when you leave him alone. Leaving the pup alone should be built up over a period of time, starting by going from one room to the next. Leaving the television on will help, as the pup feels he has company. Remember, your puppy has come from a pack; he has never known loneliness. He has lived his life, up to now, with his mother and littermates. He will howl or cry for them as soon as he is on his own, yelling for them to come and find him, as he would in the wild.

SOCIALISATION

It is essential to socialise Poodles with other animals as soon as possible. This is easily done with the young pup. My Poodles are mixed with cats, horses, sheep and cows on excursions out and about. They are walked in towns and along roads to become accustomed to traffic. I take them along to my local garden centre from the age of ten weeks where they meet lots of children, people in wheelchairs, other dogs, animals, birds and much activity.

Because of his natural inclination to chase anything, the Poodle must be taught some basic exercises of Come, Drop/Down and Stay, so that he will stop with a command from you before ever an undesirable chase gets under way. Those moving to a country area with an older dog will have to introduce the dog to new contacts. Try to choose animals, such as horses, that are used to having dogs around so that they will not panic and flee. Put the dog on a lead, take him into the paddock and go through his basic exercises of Sit and Stay and Come. Do the same with other animals, though do not enter a field of free-roaming cows, as they are quite likely to herd. And do get permission from the owners to enter fields of animals.

I once had a Poodle in for re-homing because he killed a cat. This dog had never been properly introduced to cats and had, by a rather irresponsible owner, been encouraged to chase cats. After a week of socialization, he went to live happily in a household with several cats! Dogs chase naturally. This instinct must be encouraged to include only those things we agree to, such as a ball.

Take your puppy out and about with you as often as possible, to meet other people, friends, dogs, children, and see traffic, etc. As we discussed before, garden centres and supermarket car parks are a good place to see life going on. You should also attend puppy socialisation classes. These give a good grounding for puppies for later in life, and you can both have fun.

A well socialised Poodle will take all new situations in his stride.

EARLY TRAINING

Teach your eight-week old pup to come. The habit is easily formed. Before you feed give a short whistle or make a sound. I go 'oo ooo' in a sing-song voice, then I give food. When the pup is not looking, do your whistle or sound, and as soon as he comes running give the food or treat. Your Poodle will quickly learn that coming to your sound brings a wonderful reward. Coming when called becomes a habit. Don't scold when the pup doesn't come. Wait and then try again. Do not give a treat unless earned by good response.

Another good way is to give your sound – whistle or 'oo ooo' – and then run away. The pup will run after you as his leader. The reward will be to get to eat a tasty treat, or lots of praise. I play hide and seek with my puppies, hiding in other rooms behind the doors, or hiding behind bushes in the garden. It doesn't really matter if he sees you hide, he will still have great fun. Later you can hide things for him to find, and he will chase and retrieve a ball. This is a wonderful way to expend excess energy in the growing dog before serious training. It is pointless trying to train a dog that is in a hyperactive frame of mind. Run off the energy, and then put in the work. Poodles are very responsive and will learn quickly how to get praise.

Although we will discuss food in the next chapter, it is as well to say that many Poodles do not cope well with high protein diets and may become extremely unsettled and agitated, making training difficult. The best action for bad behaviour is time out. Ignore the dog and walk away, game and association over. Leave the dog alone for a short time. A dog being disregarded for misbehaviour is the greatest punishment required based on

GROOMING AND HANDLING

Your puppy needs to get used to being groomed and handled from an early age.

Accustom your puppy to being brushed.

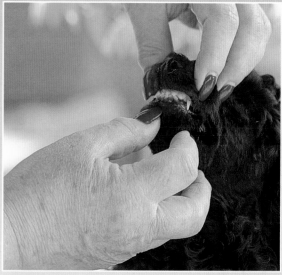

Open his mouth and examine the teeth and gums.

Pick up the front paws in turn.

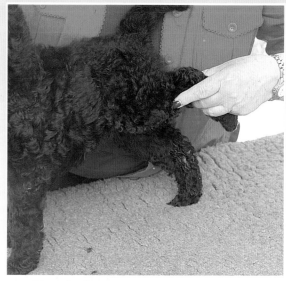

Now lift each of the back legs.

THE BEST OF CARE

When buying a puppy there are several aspects of rearing to be considered regardless of his intended role in life. All Poodles, whether friend or working companion, will perform to a higher standard as well as be more contented and good natured if they are happy and well. Sensible feeding on a natural diet will do much to retain a peaceable, tranquil nature, as will a few other considerations.

Dogs need to be fed because we control them. They cannot search for their food. Indeed, when they can get out into the garden to eat earth – with its natural nutrients – they are usually told not to do it. We are more concerned for the look of the posh grass, or flower beds than we are about our pets taking in what consists of natural supplements to them.

Dogs need a secure environment, including suitable sleeping quarters (even if this is on our bed). We have to provide this, as they are restricted from seeking their own. Puppies need time and attention from the moment you acquire them. They also need some form of protection against infectious diseases. Poodles need to have their hair/coat looked after. People/owners must be aware that there are certain illnesses, hereditary or otherwise, auto-immune, genetic, congenital, viral, that Poodles may suffer, as with any other breed of dog. Owners have a responsibility to try to ensure that their dogs' basic needs are met.

NUTRITION
It would be easy to write a whole book on the subject of diet. I suggest any dog owner get hold of a copy of Juliette de Bairacli Levy's book *The Complete Herbal Handbook for the Dog and Cat*, *Give a Dog a Bone* by Australian Vet, Dr. Ian Billinghurst and *Feeding Dogs the Natural Way* by Christopher Day.

A BALANCED DIET
A dog needs the right balance of nutrients in his diet if he is to thrive in life. These include:
- **Protein:** Protein is needed for growth, maintenance and repair. It is found in meat, dairy products, fish and eggs, as well as vegetables, pulses, cereals and other sources. It is important to give a variety of these foods in order to supply all the amino acids the dog requires to sustain good health.
- **Carbohydrates:** These are found in fruit and vegetables. Refined and less desirable forms come from biscuits and rice.

The aim is to feed a well balanced diet suited to your Poodle's age and lifestyle.

- **Fats:** Fats provide energy and are primarily used for muscular effort and for the production of various types of body tissue. They are essential in the make-up of cellular membranes and for the production of hormones. Unsaturated fats (or good fats containing 'fatty acids') are needed for the body, skin and coat and are provided from oily fish such as sardines, some vegetable sources and uncooked oils.

  Saturated fats are found in animal and dairy products and are considered to be harmful in large amounts, but essential to a balanced diet. The body needs both.
- **Water:** Water must be available at all times and changed at least daily.

COMMERCIAL OR HOME-COOKED DIET

The Poodle is not a fussy eater, unless he is ill, has an allergy to a food substance, or has been taught to be by his owner.

Therefore, what your Poodle is fed is down to the owner's personal choice. However, whatever feeding regime you adopt, you should be sure to do your research and check that it is a nutritionally balanced diet for your dog that will promote good health and energy.

"You are what you eat", so the saying goes. This is also true of the Poodle to a degree. Food needs to be considered and understood. Not all foods suit all dogs. For many owners it is a seemingly easy option to feed dry 'complete' food, and some dogs appear to do well on this. Other owners feed tinned food and are happy with the result.

However, if we saw what is claimed to be included in some of our pet's processed food under the label 'animal derivatives' we would probably feel quite sick and never buy processed dog food again, whether dry complete, tinned or otherwise. If you choose to feed commercially prepared dog food,

try to choose the best you can afford, going for natural, organic ingredients where possible.

If you feed any size Poodle on a natural diet, you will at least know what is going into the dog. Raw meaty bones are a good way to start. Poodles of all sizes relish them. I stress *raw*. Cooked bones are altered, will splinter and become dangerous. Cooked bones of any sort must *not* be given to dogs.

Any chopped vegetable, raw or slightly cooked, for which some dogs have a preference, are excellent. These include broccoli (my Poodles love the flower tops and the stalks), swede, which is a favourite, and turnips, carrot and spinach. Raw cabbage is excellent, as are yams or sweet potatoes. Vegetables can be easily chopped or shredded in a food processor and added to meat, three or four times a week. A small Poodle will need only a mixture of about one level tablespoon and a large Poodle about two tablespoons.

DIETARY CHOICES

Canned food, fed with biscuit.

Complete diet which does not need additional supplements.

A homemade diet of fresh meat which can be fed with vegetables and wholemeal bread.

Meat is best fed raw. This is, after all, natural for the dog, which is descended from the wolf and from whom the dog has inherited his general construction, constitution and make-up. I use beef on occasions, lamb, chicken, turkey and unbleached tripe, all easily available in neat packs from the butcher or pet store and stored in the home freezer. When you feed today, take tomorrow's meat out and place in refrigerator to thaw, though dogs prefer food that is not too cold. What could be simpler? Most dog owners cook the dog's meat because they hate the thought of eating raw meat themselves, but for the dog, nothing could be more natural.

Apart from vegetables, eggs and bits of cheese and fruit (my Poodles love apples) a sensible diet for an adult dog consists of raw meaty bones (after a walk) or wholemeal bread and salt-free butter, or some soaked holistic biscuit (up to a mugful for the larger Poodles, a tablespoon for the small ones).

For dinner, at about 4-5 o'clock, my dogs have meat, which includes tripe, lamb, breast of lamb with bones, turkey or chicken. I feed about 1 lb (approx 0.5 kg) or more for the Standards and 3-4 ounces (85-113 g) for the small ones, with vegetables. I never mix biscuit with the meat as it tends to ferment, which can cause dangerous gas in the stomach. It is certainly not a good idea to feed a large dog only once a day. Large dogs with a deep rib cage can bloat (known as Gastric Torsion) when fed one large meal of meat and biscuit or one large meal of complete food. Bloat is dangerous, extremely painful and frequently results in death.

FOODS TO AVOID

Chocolate is highly toxic to dogs and has been known to kill them. Other foods to avoid include onions, grapes and raisins, macadamia nuts and avocado. It is also worth remembering that other foods can be toxic if eaten in large enough quantities, such as broccoli.

ADDITIVES AND VITAMINS

My dogs have Brewers Yeast tablets (from the Health store) daily. You can give up to six a day, depending on the size of the dog. They also have flax oil, which is rich in Omega three. Puppies and pregnant bitches have the addition of slippery elm powder (a marvellous food for preventing bad tummies as well as giving great nourishment). Garlic is a food which is beneficial for cleansing the system, worming, and as a healer or as an aid to prevent infection.

Vitamins should not be needed if the quality of the food is good. Over-supplementation, as well as lack of vitamins, can cause disorders, so the balance has to be correct. Although vitamins and minerals are added to some processed foods, these are not always natural and therefore they are not easily assimilated by dogs.

WHOLEFOODS

Holistic dog biscuit is now available and is certainly, in my opinion, the best.

I feed my adult dogs twice a da. I give my own cereal mix or holistic or organic dog biscuit (partially soaked for pups) in the morning and meat with raw vegetables for dinner in the early evening. Puppies have four meals a day from eight weeks and three meals from sixteen weeks or so, depending on the pup's growth and need.

FOOD INTOLERANCE

It must be noted that there are dogs of all breeds that are highly intolerant of 'gluten', which is found in wheat, barley, oats and rye. A dog with gluten intolerance will get bouts of diarrhoea, painful colic or even fits when fed this form of protein in food. Watch out for the first sign of unhappiness or discomfort in a pup or dog and discontinue feeding biscuit meal, which includes all dry meal. As an alternative, you could use well-cooked wholemeal rice, which is a grass and is naturally

PUPPY CAUTION

It is important not to over-exercise young, growing bones. The larger the variety of Poodle, the more care must be taken. Over-exercise may result in lameness. Often, a dog will grow out of this, but it is better to take care rather than (literally) pay for the consequences of lasting damage. That does not mean wrapping your Poodle in cotton wool or not allowing plenty of free running exercise.

gluten free. Even better is millet and/or quinoa, cooked into porridge, or flaked and fed raw mixed with meat or milk. You could also use vegetables or buy gluten-free meal.

OBESITY

Just as with humans, too much food and/or too little exercise can result in your Poodle becoming overweight, which carries with it all sorts of health problems. Check with the vet if you think your dog has put on weight suddenly, in case there is a problem. Otherwise cut down on the food. A Poodle that has

been neutered may put on weight more easily, so diet and exercise may need to be more controlled. Older dogs may need a reduction in food if they are less mobile.

EXERCISE

Ideally, your Poodle should be walked twice a day. Once a day should be considered the bare minimum. If you walk your Poodle twice a day you should aim for about half an hour of exercise each time, less for a young puppy. Poodles of all sizes love to run. They need to use up their excess energy as much as any other breed. The general rule for your Poodle's daily routine is: free running, chasing a ball, play, a moderate amount of training (such as sitting before the ball is thrown and sitting on return of fetch), a walk on the lead, cuddles and praise, feeding. This will help to ensure that you have a sensible, well-adjusted Poodle with a calm attitude and a warm, loving heart. One small or short walk first thing in the morning and then no further exercise spells boredom, excess energy and frustration.

GROOMING

COAT CARE

All Poodles must have their hair/coat brushed and combed daily or at least four to five times a week. You will need a slicker brush, a wire-claw type brush for parts of the body that are not clipped, and a metal-toothed comb that will enable you to comb the hair through from the root to remove dead hair and prevent mats forming. A table with non-slip mat to put the dog on is an asset.

Brush your puppy from day one, gently going over the entire coat. A couple of minutes a day will save hours of time later on. When the coat is changing from puppy to adult, grooming will become more arduous, with the fluffy puppy hair coming out to be replaced with coarser, denser hair. Once the change is complete the coat will be easier to groom, but it will still need regular brushing and combing.

Try to have a consistent routine during grooming so that areas are less likely to be missed. Start with the head when brushing, combing and bathing; grooming away from the eyes, down the ears, behind the ears. Assuming the body hair is clipped, brush the front legs, then comb, carry on to the back legs, and then the tail. Be sure to lift hair to part it and comb from the root, close to the skin, outwards.

Your Poodle will need to be clipped on a regular four to six week basis; more if he is to be entered into competitions. Usually a professional groomer is required, unless the owner learns the skill.

Poodle coats need constant attention. Pet owners almost invariably skimp on brushing their dogs, which then come into the grooming salon every six weeks or so with mats and

A game with a ball combines mental stimulation with physical exercise.

tangles in their coat. Once upon a time, the only considerate and kind way to deal with such felted mats was to get underneath the mat with a fine blade and clip it off. With today's many preparations, conditioners and mat-breakers, the groomer has a wider choice and more capacity to sort out a neglected coat. However, the

prime consideration must be to the dog and if the best solution is to clip off the coat, then this must be done. It will grow again. If you brush and comb your Poodle on a regular basis, his coat will always look smart, even after a dig in the garden or getting thoroughly muddy. Once dry, the coat will brush out marvellously.

71

GROOMING

If you take on a Poodle, you must commit the time to regular grooming sessions, even if you are keeping your dog in a pet trim.

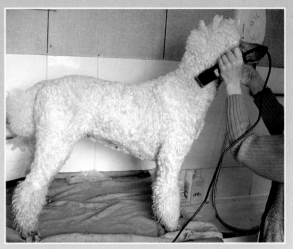

Your Poodle will need to be clipped every four to six weeks.

The nails can be trimmed using guillotine type nail clippers.

If you are worried about using nail clippers, you can file the nails.

Hair that grows inside the ears needs to be removed.

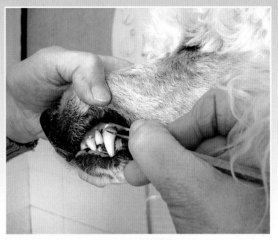

If tartar accumulates on the teeth it will need to be removed using a tooth scaler, or a toothbrush and specially formulated toothpaste.

NAILS

Nails are usually best left to the groomer to cut or grind, although you can learn to do this yourself (ask your vet to show you how). There are different types of nail clippers including guillotine, scissor or straight. Nails have a 'quick' (the nail's blood and nerve supply) running through them and cutting this will cause profuse bleeding. It is also very painful, so be careful to only nip off a small amount at a time if you need to do this yourself. Better still and safer, use a nail grinder or emery board. Pet owners can file their pet's nails without worry of cutting the quick.

EARS

The Poodle grows hair inside the ears as well as outside. It is part of the grooming procedure to deal with this. An experienced groomer should show a novice how to do this painlessly, by lifting the flap of the ear against the head (thereby protecting the inner ear) and holding the muzzle to keep the dog still, then using forceps or thumb and forefinger to tease out a few hairs at a time. It is always a good idea to use some ear powder first as this will help to loosen the hair. Where brown wax is evident, mites have probably invaded, so clean the ear with alcohol, lemon juice or ear cleaner and apply ear powder before and after removing as much of the offending mess as possible. This may need to be a daily procedure until the problem has cleared up.

TEETH

My dogs never need their teeth cleaning – they chew bones and this does the job. However, teeth need to be checked and if necessary, cleaned with toothpaste specially formulated for dogs, or, where an accumulation of tartar has formed, cleaned with a tooth scale or scraper. There is also an additive to remove tartar that can be sprinkled into the feed. Provided teeth are kept clean there should not be any necessity for veterinary attention.

BATHING

Poodles are bathed regularly – either by the professional groomer, or by the owner wishing to keep the dog clean and/or to compete in dog shows. Most show Poodles are bathed every 7-10 days. Pet dogs are bathed usually every 4-6 weeks. The smaller Poodle will fit into a large sink. The Standard Poodle will need to be put into a bath or

A Poodle will soon get used to the routine of being bathed.

large shower basin. Either way, a spray is essential for wetting the hair and thoroughly rinsing. It makes life considerably easier if the bath is at waist height beside the grooming table, which is less strenuous on one's back.

Always use a good quality shampoo formulated for dogs. You will also need a quality conditioner; some of which can be left in the coat while others are rinsed out. All mats and tangles must be removed before bathing, as the wet hair will clog more to the felts and make drying extremely difficult.

Stand the dog in the bath; wet the hair thoroughly with warm water, working from the head downwards. Working from the base of the hair outwards on long hair to be sure of getting all the

hair wet. Distribute the diluted (where necessary) shampoo evenly and rub in with fingertips, systematically, as with grooming. Work the shampoo through the coat carefully to avoid breaking the long coat on show dogs.

Rinse the coat very thoroughly making sure all the shampoo is removed before applying the conditioner. Work this through the coat and rinse. Be sure to rinse well underneath, too.

Anyone contemplating bathing the Poodle on a regular basis will be well advised to buy a proper dog dryer. Expensive they may seem, but they save hours of time and allow for two hands to be free to hold and brush the coat, blow-drying as you go.

Towel the coat after bathing. Turn on the dryer and brush the

coat from the foot upwards, layering each section until the hair is dry and fluffy. After drying, comb through with a wide-tooth comb.

The show dog will need to lie on his side so that his mane can be brushed in layers as it is blown dry. Brush from the skin outwards, taking small strands of coat at a time. For this a pin brush may be more proficient, without breaking the hair or dragging too much out. If the coat is not thoroughly dry it will curl and make scissoring more difficult.

Some groomers like to use a 'blaster' to remove excess water from the coat before drying commences. This may save on towels and save time, but it is not an essential expense to purchase this piece of equipment.

CLIPPING AND SCISSORING

There are many good clippers on the market today. It is a good idea to buy the best and I recommend getting in touch with a good grooming equipment outlet for a catalogue to enable you to see what is on offer. Another good way to find out more about grooming is to attend one of the marvellous 'Grooming Road Shows' that go around the country, as advertised in the weekly dog papers.

There are several retail outlets for grooming equipment, including scissors, which are quite a personal item and come in many prices. The professional groomer will have many pairs of scissors for different trimming,

HOW TO TRIM YOUR POODLE

Clip up each toe in turn.

Clip from under the eye towards the muzzle.

Clip one-third of the hair on the tail from the base.

but for the novice or pet owner trimming their own dog, one pair will suffice to begin with. Try the different scissors and see which suits you. These are available from retail outlets, at dog shows and grooming seminars.

There is a lot of scissor work to be done on a Poodle and only practise will allow the groomer to achieve a smooth, almost satin finish to the well cared for coat. Finishing is an art that some excel in more than others. Different scissors give different finishes and the groomer must try several pairs of scissors in order to find the pair that is right for them. Most sales outlets are happy to help you choose the right type. Scissors vary in price and in order to sustain the outstanding presentation that some groomers achieve, it is imperative to buy quality products, such as clippers and scissors as well as shampoo and finishing sculpture conditioner. It

really does make a difference and the investment is worthwhile.

Finishing is achieved by literally skimming over the coat with the scissors accurately placed to edge the coat. As the Poodle coat constantly grows and moves and has a natural tendency to curl despite straightening conditioners, this finish will not last, but still the dog will look expertly smart.

Good scissoring is an art. It is fascinating to watch groomers from different parts of the world scissoring in their own style to achieve perfection. By attending grooming seminars you can see this interesting skill in action and will see that different groomers have their individual styles. Some fluff the hair outwards and let it fall before commencing scissoring, and some comb it upwards. Some will say one way is the only correct way, but I have seen dogs turned out to sheer perfection both ways.

The same goes for how you hold a pair of scissors. Some use thumb and index, some thumb and middle finger, and some thumb and fourth finger. I try all ways and don't see any difference! There's probably no hope for me! Though I do like scissors with a guard.

TRIMMING STYLES
- **Sporting:** The easiest clip to manage for the pet Poodle is the sporting trim, or as it is sometimes called, the utility trim. Here the feet and face are clipped as usual and the body clipped with a coarser blade to leave about enough hair to give the appearance of close wool or astrakhan. The lower part of the leg is left longer to give an elegant look, with bracelets or socks. These are trimmed to an oval shape with scissors.
- **Lamb trim:** This is the next most popular trim with pet

POODLE

Sporting/Utility trim.

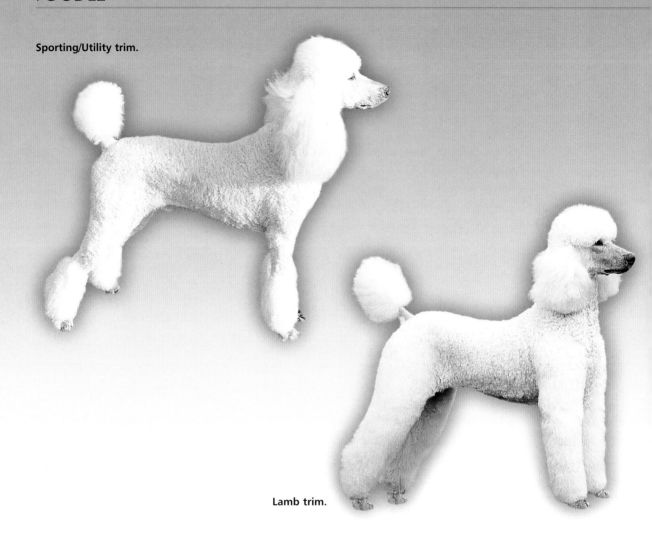

Lamb trim.

owners. Here the feet and face are clipped as normal, the body is clipped with a coarser blade and the legs are trimmed into trousers with scissors.

- **Puppy clip:** This is a style used for puppies up to four or five months of age for the pet Poodle, or up to one year for the show dog. The feet, face and tail are clipped as normal. The body hair is kept long, but is sculpted into an attractive shape with the scissors.

- **Puppy lion:** This is the next stage of styling for the show dog. The coat from the last rib is cut to a shorter length with scissors, with the back leg being shaped with the contours of the joints. The front legs are neatened and shaped into the chest hair. The puppy lion is an artistic style, which requires expertise and involves much work to perfect.

- **Lion:** This trim takes an expert to perfect. The feet, face and base of tail are clipped as normal, the front legs are clipped from the elbow to just above the wrist joint, leaving a mane of hair on the chest that is sculpted into a ball with scissors. The back legs have three bracelets, which are trimmed into shape with scissors.

- **Continental:** This is the second most popular trim for the show dog. The feet, face, base of tail and front legs are clipped as for the Lion trim, with the mane shaped into a ball. However, the back legs are shaved close to the lower bracelet (hock joint) and a round, sculpted ring of hair is left on the hip bone.

HOW TO GROOM YOUR POODLE

Certainly the Poodle is the most intriguing of all breeds to trim as he has so many styles into which his unique, non-moulting coat can be artistically contoured. Coming in three sizes, the Poodle is one of the most versatile of all breeds, but he will happily revert back to his origin of a water retriever at a moment's notice. So his clip will vary according to his lifestyle.

In this example, I have used the Standard Poodle to demonstrate, as it is easier to see the detail. However, all sizes are trimmed the same. With all styles, the Poodle will need to have his feet, face and tail clipped. We will deal with this first. There are certain rules to observe. Apart from the feet, always use clippers with the growth of coat. Where the face is concerned, always clip away from the eye. Unless you are experienced using clippers, it is quite likely that you will need time to get round all the delicate clipped parts of the Poodle, so use clipper lubricant frequently, every five minutes or so, and check the blade of the clipper for heat by putting it on your face. As soon as it feels more than a little warm, change the blade. *Dogs have been burned with hot blades and it takes a long time for them to regain their confidence.*

FEET

Blade No 15 Oster or a 30 for a closer finish on the dark colours. Starting at the rear right foot (being sure the dog is standing square and is comfortable) hold the leg beneath the hock joint, just above the foot, taking care the foot is underneath the dog and not pulled out to the side. Gently press open the toes with your fingers and clip the hair away from around the nails, flexing the wrist to turn the clipper, rather than the dog's foot. Clip up each toe in turn, taking the hair from between the toes and being careful to avoid ramming the clipper into the web. Clip to the base of the toe and no higher, or you will spoil the finish and give the Poodle what is known as a chicken look. Clip each foot in turn. If the blade gets too warm, change it.

FACE

For pet dogs use a Blade No 10 Oster, or equivalent. Show dogs are clipped closer, more frequently with a No 15 or 30. Keep the blade as flat as possible, but without putting undue pressure on the skin. Hold the dog's muzzle in the right hand, folding the ear back over the head, and clip from the corner of the eye to the upper corner of the ear in a straight, neat line. Clip under the eye to the inner corner, then from between the eyes (at the stop) down to tip of nose. Now clip from under the eye towards the muzzle, to the nose. Repeat on the other side of face.

From the base of the ear, clip down to the point of the throat, the adam's apple. Clip the chin from the edge of the mouth to the nose, taking care to tighten loose skin at all times.

For the show Poodle the neck is clipped into a U-shape, shaving the hair down to an inch or two above the breastbone, depending on style of mane and the emphasis required to show off the length of the neck.

TAIL

No 15 Oster or equivalent. Clip one third of the tail from the base, leaving enough hair to create a pompom. With the undocked tail the same amount is clipped from the base, and then tailored with the scissors. Clip under the tail with a No 10 blade, being careful not to use clippers on the bulge of the anus.

BODY

Lamb trim: No 5 or 7 Oster or equivalent. Clip from the base of the head, just beneath the ears, down the top and underneath the neck. Lift the leg and clip under the arm and along the chest to the groin. Clip the neck to just above shoulder level, then move along the back to the base of tail and just above the hip. Then move along and down, over the rib cage to the groin. Clip underneath, covering the stomach and the groin, carefully taking hair from around the nipples and genitals (always holding the delicate parts as you go to ensure safety).

POODLE

The Dutch trim is rarely seen in the show ring.

Sporting or Utility: Using a No 5 or No 7 Oster, clip the neck from the base of the head, move down over the shoulder, down the back to the tail, and then down and along the ribcage, under the chest, stomach and groin area. Clip the back legs, inside and out, to an inch above the hock joint. Then, with an eye line to balance, clip the inside and out of the front legs to the same level.

Bath and dry as for the Lamb trim. Scissor the topknot as for the Lamb trim. Comb outwards and then scissor the bracelets into an oval shape. Trim the tail as for the Lamb trim.

Dutch: Rarely is this old-fashioned clip seen today. Using a No 10 Oster, clip under the neck to the point of the breastbone and on top to about 5 cm (2 inches) above the withers. Taking a direct line, shave a blade's width between the shoulders, across the withers, continuing the line to the base of the tail. Clip the abdomen from groin to navel and then progress downwards, incorporating the insides of the thighs.

Brush through the entire unclipped coat. Bath and blow dry as for the Lamb trim. Go over the clipped part on the body to ensure a tidy finish. Scissor the top and tail as for the Lamb trim. Scissor the back legs to a neat finish, leaving a pronounced curve at the edge of the clipped parts. Scissor the front, leaving a pronounced curve.

Brush through the remaining hair, trousers, topknot and tail, removing all tangles with a slicker brush and wide-tooth comb. Where necessary, to prevent causing too much discomfort, use the mat-breaker. Anti-tangle conditioner can also be used.

Bathe your Poodle in a suitable, natural, enhancing shampoo, such as tea tree and lavender, or use a protein coat-strengthening formula with consideration to colour and condition of coat. Use a quality conditioner, such as sculpture finish, to aid scissoring.

Blow dry the coat, brushing all the time in sections, from bottom of leg upwards, using a pin or slicker brush. Bathing the hair will lift it slightly, so tidy any clipped areas where necessary by going over with same depth blade as before.

Hem by scissoring round the bottom of leg hair. Feet should only barely be seen. Scissor the legs going with the contours of the limbs, using a silhouette line, with scissors pointing downwards or upwards but never crossways (apart from when hemming). Start from the bottom of the leg and keep the line going to the top, then take the next line and repeat the process. Finally, skim across the hair to blend in.

Holding the muzzle, comb the hair forward and scissor the topknot across the eye, upwards. Comb the hair to the left and trim across the top of the ears and the back of the neck, then repeat on right side. Trim over the top, taking care to leave a nice top but being sure the dog can see clearly.

GROOMING THE SHOW DOG

If you want to show, it is essential for you to be able to bath, clip and groom your Poodle yourself, otherwise the procedure will be very expensive. Trimming a pet is one thing; turning out a show dog is something else entirely and takes many people years to perfect. Luckily Poodle people are generally very kind and helpful. Breeders and expert trimmers can, and do, help novice exhibitors with their trimming. The best advice is to watch, listen and learn. In time you will, hopefully, be trimming as well as the best.

It is a good idea to have a professional photograph of a dog in show trim on the wall when you start scissoring the mane and legs of your Poodle and try to copy it. Remember, no artist ever painted a masterpiece the first time he picked up a paintbrush. It will take time, sweat and tears to perfect scissoring skills, unless you are extremely blessed.

Your Poodle show dog will need brushing every day, or at least three or four times a week, depending on his individual coat and whether or not he is at the age (between ten and fourteen months) when his coat is changing from puppy to adult. If you brush the dog every day, your task of growing the coat will be easier. Brush each strand of hair carefully. To do this lay your Poodle on his side and start brushing at the bottom of the ribcage. Part layers with a tail comb or your fingers and brush

Time, skill and patience are required if you want to keep a Poodle in Show trim.

the hair downwards. Comb each layer until you reach the spine; include the neck hair, top and ears. Then turn your dog over and start the other side. I often do this sitting on the floor watching television, the dog relaxed in front of me. If you have attended shows you will have seen Poodles being groomed this way. All dogs are thoroughly groomed before they go into the show ring.

MATS
De-matting tangles that have formed overnight on a dog going through a coat change requires care. Often, it is more beneficial to split the hair with your fingers. Wet hair is more pliable and not quite so susceptible to breakage. Comb with a wide-tooth comb, never a fine one.

Use a good conditioner if the coat is dry. Apply this from the bottom of the ribcage up, parting the hair as you go to ensure all the layers are conditioned and the solution has not just run over the top. It is possible to get 'stay-in' conditioner. When preparing a coat for the show ring, use the conditioner without oil and rinse.

GROWING HAIR
As the hair grows, the ear fringes will need protecting and maybe the topknot and neck hair. The hair must be kept out of the dog's eyes at all times, or you will have a dog with constantly running eyes. As soon as the puppy's hair is long enough, tie it up with a rubber band. When the hair gets a little bit longer, you can use ponytail ties or wrappers.

Ear fringes can be wrapped,

TO OIL OR NOT TO OIL

When people ask me whether they should oil their Poodle, especially through coat change, I have to be rather non-committal – it really does depend on the coat. I have oiled coats with non-satisfactory results (especially white coats) and I have oiled coats with good results

Poodles that have their coats oiled need to be bathed on a regular basis – every 7-10 days. Oil does help to prevent matting – if the coat is mat free to start with – and grooming is less essential. But the oiled coat collects more dirt with the danger of breakage and itching, and it can be extremely messy on the furniture. In general, the coat is far easier to handle and grow when it is clean. Dirty hair is more brittle. If you want to grow a show coat then every care must be taken to keep the hair clean, healthy and free from mats or tangles.

being careful to ensure that the ear leather (the flesh part of the ear) is free from any bands. You can use polythene or cotton wrappers but make absolutely sure your Poodle gets used to these when you are around. Until the dog has become accustomed to having these strange things on his ears, take them off when you are not around. Some dogs grasp wrappers in their mouths and chew them off, with disastrous results. They can chew the hair off with it and may ingest the wrapper.

Show dogs must have their fun regardless of coat. Exercise is essential to a healthy life and bones are essential to clean healthy teeth. Use old socks with the toes cut out to pull over your dog's bracelets when he is chewing on bones. The topknot can be protected with a snood.

THE FULL PUPPY CLIP
- Clip the face feet and tail.
- Thoroughly groom the coat with a slicker or pin brush and a wide-tooth comb.
- Clip under the tummy/abdomen from the groin to the navel with a No 10 blade.
- Bathe in a suitable shampoo for the colour and condition of coat and apply a quality conditioner to aid scissor work.
- Blow dry the hair away from the body, lifting with a pin brush to ensure it does not curl.
- Trim round the bottom of the legs to allow a peep at the toes.
- Scissor very fine ends from hair to an even and dense-looking finish. As the coat grows in length, scissor slightly shorter at base of tail, blending the hair up towards the body to

obtain an effective, easy on the eye, glamorous shape. Scissor the tail as for Lamb.

A lot of time and effort goes into maintaining this style. It is mostly seen on puppies in the North American show ring, although there are some pet owners who adore their Poodles in this stunning trim and are happy to pay for the time and expertise the groomer takes in turning out an evenly scissored finish.

THE PUPPY LION
Sometimes, this is called the T clip, although it is not strictly as acute as the Scandinavian outline.
- Clip the feet, face and tail.
- Groom and bath as for the Puppy trim.
- Clip abdomen area.
- Feel the body to locate the last

Puppy Clip.

Puppy Lion trim.

Photo: Martin Leigh

rib. For the novice it is a good idea to put a narrow bandage around the dog at just below this point to distinguish an even line and to be sure that the balance is right. (Roughly one third is trimmed shorter while two thirds is left for the mane).

- Cut with the scissors held straight, up the edge of your line or bandage from the near side, up one side, over body and down the other side. This is more easily achieved when the dog is standing square with its bottom towards you.

- Remove your 'guide line' bandage.
- Scissor the back legs to an even length, taking in consideration of rear angulations, which are accentuated. Once you are well practised with scissors and have a good eye, copy the trimming from an up-to-date photograph.
- Flick the mane with the comb, allow the dog to shake and the hair to settle, then scissor round, rather like skimming over the coat, keeping scissors level, to achieve a blend where mane meets shorter back hair

to enhance the appearance of a well defined neck.
- Shape round mane, shaping incline from brisket up towards ear.
- Scissor the front legs into a tubular shape, moulding or sculpturing to blend where they join the mane at elbow. Scissor the tail as for the Lamb trim.

TRADITIONAL LION
This is also known as the full pack or English Saddle.
- Clip the feet, face and tail.
- Groom, bath, condition and

blow the hair dry as for the Puppy trim.

- You should already have the coat parted behind the rib cage as in the Puppy Lion. If not, do this. It is always advisable to clip the mane in before the back end to make it easier to achieve a good balance. Again, a bandage can be used for forming lines. This is always a good idea as you can tie it around at the given points and move it up or down to achieve a balance before putting your scissors in. Once you've snipped, there is no turning back!

Traditional Lion.

- Apply the bandage about two inches (10cm) above the wrist, (the first joint above the foot) and look to see if this will allow you to scissor an oval bracelet. Cut above the bandage line, clip with No 10 up the front leg to remove the hair up to the joint of the elbow. Do not clip over the elbow. Trim the bracelet by combing out and clipping the ends to an oval shape.
- Scissor round the bottom of the mane to achieve a ball finish.
- On the back leg, feel for hock joint (first joint above back foot) and apply the bandage about one inch above.
- Feel for the stifle (knee) joint and apply the second bandage just above to define. Stand back and check that there is a good balance between the three defined points. Move the bandage slightly up or down until you feel happy that the dog looks right. With the scissors, cut a thin line above the bandage. These points can be carefully clipped, or more defined with scissors. When starting on the other leg do check that your lines correspond from behind.
- Comb the hair upwards and allow it to settle. Scissor each section to a smooth rounded finish.
- Scissor the tail as for the Lamb.

CONTINENTAL LION TRIM

Most of the Poodles shown in the USA are trimmed in this style at 12 months of age. In the UK, this

Continental Lion.

trim is less seen now than it used to be, as the Kennel Club does not demand it. Certainly it takes less time than the Traditional or Puppy, but there is still a lot of work here to make it as beautiful as it should look. The idea of the clip – apart from tradition – is to show off the Poodle's good angles as much as possible. This trim is mostly seen on the Standard Poodle, though favoured in countries such as Japan in all three sizes.

- Clip the feet, face and tail, bath, condition and blow the hair dry as for the Puppy trim.
- Cut in the front end (mane) as for the Lion, including scissoring to finish.
- For beginners it is a good idea to place a saucer on the hip joint to define a rosette. Take the scissors and cut round the saucer. Remove the saucer and you will reveal a large rosette. Depending on whether the dog is longer in back than it should be, or perfectly proportioned, the saucer can be moved backward or forward to achieve the best balance before cutting commences.
- With No 10 blade, start clipping from a position just above the hock joint and clip up to your newly made rosette. Clip round this, being careful not to clip the rosette itself. Clip the narrow area between the end of mane and the rosette. Lifting the hair with the comb, scissor round the rosette to achieve a smart round puff of hair.
- Trim the tail as for other trims.

SUMMARY

There is a lot to consider when taking on a Poodle, which is why this magnificent breed is not for everyone. However, your hard work, time and effort will be rewarded by the devotion of your Poodle. You get back what you put in. Feed your Poodle well, exercise him regularly, care for his coat and occupy his mind and you will be rewarded by a healthy, happy, affectionate and entertaining companion.

TRAINING AND SOCIALISATION

6 Chapter

P oodles of all sizes are very easy to train. In fact they are so easy and so intelligent that they train US very well! Such is their sweetness, one look is enough to melt us and we give way. However, with a little thought, kindness and a few treats the Poodle can be taught to be wonderfully obedient.

A Poodle pup between the ages of 8 and 16 weeks can be taught many exercises by using our body and hands to convey messages. Back this up with praise and a tasty treat here and there and you will end up with an amazingly bright and obedient dog with the spirit of a clown that will be a sheer delight to own. Treats, when used to reinforce good behaviour, help to cement a bond between us.

YOUR ROLE
Your role is to realise that all dogs

You need to establish a sense of leadership so that your Poodle respects and co-operates with you.

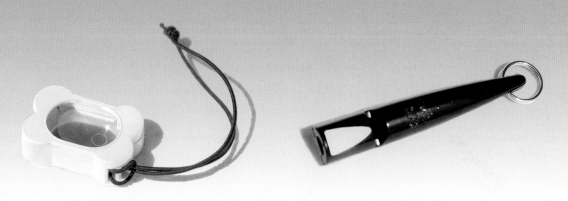

Clickers and whistles are two popular training aids.

need to follow. That does not imply that you have to be stern, or a bully; it means that you use your talents to demonstrate, encourage, then praise for response. It's as simple as that! Already you have a head start, because without you the dog won't get fed, be secure in a home and thrive. You can further this 'pack leader' role by a few thoughtful actions and a bit of confidence. Knowing how to teach certain disciplines will take you a long way to achieving everything you ever wanted from your four-legged friend. The Poodle is a great, dear and trusted friend when correctly reared. Very few Poodles that come into rescue have an attitude problem, so that speaks well of the breed's ability to cope with irregular tempered owners. Remember that dogs read shouting from humans as a sign of instability.

TRAINING EXERCISES
All puppies and dogs benefit from being trained. As well as becoming part of the family, the Poodle will thoroughly enjoy learning to do things to please you. Even five minutes a day with your dog should result in your dog learning commands such as Sit, Down and Stay, and it will also bring you closer.

As with all forms of training, take care not to over-train or over-tire your pup. Training works best when carried out in short, fun sessions. If you sense your Poodle is becoming bored, tired or frustrated, stop and try again later. Do not go on to the next exercise until the one you are working on is learned and the pup is confident and sure of the command.

TRAINING AIDS
The main rule with all training is to keep it fun and concentrate on rewarding good behaviour. Generally speaking, training aids are not strictly necessary. However, many people find that some training aids can help make the process quicker and easier.

Two popular methods include:
- **Clicker Training:** Using the clicker, a small matchbox-shaped training aid pioneered by dolphin trainer Karen Pryor, is a relatively new technique for training. It is held in the hand and clicked to mark behaviour the precise moment it happens. Some trainers have had great success having taught the dog that it will earn a treat when responding to the sound of the clicker.

  To introduce the clicker to your Poodle have a treat in your hand, press the clicker and toss a treat for him. The association is soon learned.
- **Whistle:** I love my whistle. Not being a strong whistler myself, I find dog whistles are a marvellous aid to use when, for instance, my Poodles are running along the beach. Once they are out of earshot I can use the whistle – which means a tasty treat – to alert them to me. It rarely fails. People who give their dogs treats for

The aim is to build up a fast and enthusiastic response to the "Come" command.

nothing will find training far more difficult, with the dog disinterested in what they say or do.

COME

Never chase your puppy. It may seem like fun to play this game, but it soon teaches the pup that you are prepared to run after him. This is not helpful. When you take home your eight week old pup, he will follow you everywhere and stray from your side only to go exploring or to investigate something that has attracted his attention. Take your pup for a walk in the garden, run and he will follow you, hide and he will seek you. Do try to make sure there are no other distractions at this early point.

- You can reinforce these early lessons with a treat. When the dog looks at you, move away and drop your hand to his nose level with the treat in your hand.
- We will call our dog, 'Sam'. When he starts to move towards you, say "Sam, Come".
- When the pup reaches you give him the treat and say *"Gooood dog"*.
- Repeat a few more times. Remember to say 'Come' only when the pup is on his way towards you.
- Do this about half a dozen times every day and your clever Poodle will soon get the message.
- Remember to make sure that you do not do any training when the pup has just eaten a meal. Train before feeding, never immediately afterwards.
- I always give a whistle when I feed my pups, even when they are in the nest and I am weaning them. By the time they are six weeks old they know my whistle means dinner when they come to me. They do not forget this basic association, and it is then used for life. It becomes habit. I whistle, they come.
- Distraction can interrupt the early training. Practice quietly at home, along the hall, in the garden, and then progress to different areas outside the home. If your dog spots something so interesting he must investigate – this is seen more in adolescence – and runs away when you call him, training must go back to basics. You can use a long lead with the unruly dog to prevent him running the wrong way during training.

STOP ON RECALL

Sometimes an emergency could arise, such as the dog being on the other side of the road and a car coming, when you need the dog to drop to the down position and wait. This halt when coming is also needed in some Obedience tests. This is an advanced exercise and must only be taught once the dog is well versed in the Drop/Down and Stay exercises (see below). Once you have decided, much earlier on in your early puppy play/training, which word to use, Drop or Down, keep to that word throughout. It is surprising how many people say to a dog 'Come-here', 'Sit-down' etc. Which do you want? Come, Sit, Down, Drop, Stand, Stay, Heel or Wait? Don't confuse the issue by using too many words. I will use 'Stand' and 'Drop' for this exercise.

- Stand the dog in front of you.
- Tell the dog to "Wait", walk a

The exercise to "Stop" on recall could be a lifesaver.

Work at getting an instant response to the "Sit."

couple of paces away and turn to face him.

- Call the dog, but the moment he makes a move towards you take a step forward and give the command to "Drop".
- Return to the dog immediately and give treat and praise.
- Repeat a few more times a day over the next week, and then gradually lengthen the distance you walk away to 10 paces, 20 paces, and then 30 paces.
- If the dog keeps coming after the command of 'Drop', you have gone too far, too fast. Go back to the beginning. Do not chastise. Reward for Response.

SIT

The Sit exercise is essential, especially when visitors come and you don't want the pup to jump up at them. You can teach your dog to sit and the visitor can offer him a treat to make friends with the dog under control.

- Call your dog to you.
- When he reaches you hold the treat right in front of his nose and raise your hand (not too high) just enough so that, to get the reward, the dog's head comes up and back, and the pup will naturally go into the Sit.
- Say "Sam, Sit", like a hissing Ssit.
- When the Sit is established, reward immediately with the treat.
- Repeat a few more times, then every day for a few more days and the dog will know 'Sit'.

As your Poodle becomes better at the exercise, you can slowly decrease the treats, offering them every third or so time. Do not keep repeating the command. Say it once, as the dog relaxes into the position you require, not before or after. The first few times you may see the dog thinking about the situation, but he will quickly learn – 'I go into this position when she does this signal and I get a tasty treat'.

I do not reinforce with my hand, but if you are tempted to, you must be careful where to place your hand on the dog. To push a dog into the sit you must ensure his head comes up first by raising the right hand with the treat enclosed while using the left hand to put gentle pressure on the *base* of the dog's back (where the tail is attached). This is important, as if placed higher up it will encourage the dog to move, as you will be poking him in the kidneys.

VARIATIONS ON SIT

SIT AT HEEL
- To get your pup to sit beside you as opposed to in front of you, stand in front of the dog and then call him, showing your hand signal and treat.
- When the dog nearly reaches you, turn and walk a few more paces to allow him to come alongside.
- You may need to twist your body to offer the treat in front of the pup's nose. Raise your hand to make the dog's head come up and give the treat as soon as the dog executes the sitting position, saying "Sit" as he goes into position.

SIT TO STAND
- One useful lesson for you to take on board is that, if you want the dog to move forward with you at any time, always strike off with the foot nearest to the dog (i.e. if your dog is on your left, use your left foot). This will help in further training when we want to teach the dog to stay.
- With the pup sitting at your side, place your hand containing food immediately in front of the dog's nose.
- Take a small step (left leg) forward, stimulating the dog to move up into the stand position.
- Say "Sam, Stand" and give food.
- Repeat as before.

Do try to teach Sit without touching. It is most effective and only requires a little patience to execute.

STANDING ON A TABLE
- Gently put your hand under the dog's tummy while the other hand draws the pup to the Stand with a treat placed in front of his nose.
- Say "Sam, Stand" as the dog comes up onto his legs and give praise. Poodles need to be accustomed to being groomed on a table.

WALKING TO HEEL
There is nothing worse than being dragged up the road by a large or small dog and then, when stopping to say hello to

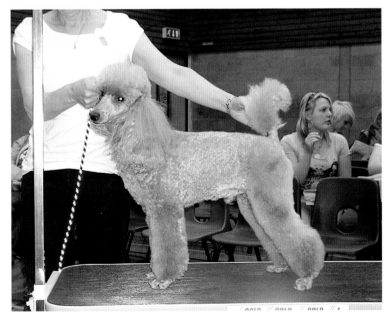

Learning to "Stand" on a table is an invaluable lesson for a dog that requires extensive grooming.

You need to get your Poodle's attention when teaching heelwork.

people, the dog jumps all over them and covers them with mud. Better to have your pal walk to heel and sit when being introduced to friends.

It is always a good idea to have a few bits of cheese or some favourite treat in your pocket when out with your dog, training or otherwise. You will need a rolled leather collar and a fairly long soft leather or nylon lead. Short leads are a complete waste of time and will merely teach the dog to pull as there would be tension on the lead at all times.

With a very young puppy it is quite easy to begin teaching exercises, including walking to heel, *without* the use of a lead. If you acquire an older dog, or an older puppy whose attention wavers and which is likely to dart off in all directions when you want to commence training, the lead will have to be attached. However, try to use the lead only as a means to an end and not to pull on as a restraint when training. The idea is for the lead to be loose, with a loop in it, to encourage your dog to walk with you without either of you tugging.

Check collars, those of steel links, are sometimes used as a training aid. These are usually unnecessary on young puppies and are quite harsh in the wrong hands. There is a knack to using a check chain and most novices don't understand that it is essential to keep a loop in the lead and only give a quick sideways check when the dog's attention wanders (before he is out of control). This check is a very quick flick with the hand and an immediate release. It is aimed to invite a quick response and alert attention. If the puppy or dog is trained properly to begin with, it is unlikely that the chain would be required. The rolled leather collar is perfectly suitable for training and as an added advantage, it doesn't break the hair of a puppy whose coat is being grown for the show ring.

Dogs look to their owners for direction. So, without too much effort and with a little forethought and organisation, a puppy can be taught the rudiments of heelwork from as young as eight weeks, by the owner moving backwards and forwards away from the pup. Certainly at this age, which is generally the time you, as a new owner, will take on the responsibility of rearing the puppy, your Poodle has realised that humans are the ones who make the rules and take care of him.

- Encourage the pup to walk at your left side with the aid of a treat held in your left hand in front of the pup at his eye level.
- Say "Sam, Heel" and walk forward a few paces, giving the dog the treat when you stop,

A group of well-behaved Poodles walking on lead.

while he is still close to your side. Initially, this can be done in your hallway or on the patio or wherever it is quiet.

- Repeat this about five times only, and then praise the pup and say "Off you go" to release him.

- Do this each day, twice a day, building up the distance and then changing the environment from house to garden, or patio to grass. The pup will be learning heel without ever having a lead put on.

- Build up to about 20 or 30 paces, and don't spend so much time repeating the exercise that your Poodle gets bored or too tired to respond efficiently. Treats can then be offered as a reminder, or to reinforce encouragement.

- Once your dog has the idea, you can walk upright with your hands relaxed or about waist level, with treat held in hand ready to give after a few paces.

- Do not give praise, or speak to your Poodle if he jumps up. Start the exercise again and be sure to praise and give a treat before the dog is encouraged by enthusiasm to jump up. Timing may be critical with a very enthusiastic dog.

- If the dog strays away from your side, call him back, take a few paces forward with him looking at you and then reward. If you move quickly when the dog's attention wanders, he will soon be alerted to you.

Once your dog has learned the word 'Heel', and what it

means, you can commence doing turns.

- First, a right turn. Use the dog's name to alert him that something different is going to happen. Say the word "Heel", and take a 180-degree turn right, patting your left leg at knee point or placing your hand with the treat at the dog's nose level the moment before executing the turn. After a few times the dog will have got the message and will enjoy this new variation.

- Then you can start on the left turn, again using a treat in your hand at the dog's eye level and warning the dog that something is about to happen by speaking his name, before turning your body 180-degrees to the left.

91

Once the dog has learned what is required it will only take a slight move of your body for him to anticipate your manoeuvres. But don't expect perfection too soon and *do* reinforce with encouragement and treats. If you get frustrated or impatient, stop for that day. Dogs learn quickly from calm, definite actions.

If you feel frustrated because the dog is not responding as you wish, stop; think over where you are going wrong. Are you moving to the next stage far too soon? Has your session gone on longer than the pup can be reasonably expected to concentrate? Does the pup want to relieve himself? Is he tired? Did you forget to run round with him chasing you to get rid of excess energy before you started training? Are you being clear and decisive with your body language and signals?

Are you meandering too much? Don't forget, you are speaking in a foreign tongue to the dog, and you must make your wishes clear in as few words as possible. Remember, dogs don't need words as much as signals.

The next step is to repeat your heel training with the lead attached. When lead training, it is important to make sure that the lead has a loop in it, so it has to be of sufficient length to allow this. The last thing you need after spending time encouraging your pup to walk beside you to heel with no lead, is to then teach him to pull by applying a short lead and having tension on the lead at all times. When first introducing the lead it is quite in order to drop the lead as soon as the puppy resists it. This should happen only a few times.

Repeat your early heelwork teaching by telling the dog to heel and giving praise and a treat. Dog-walking on a tight lead is no fun for dog or owner. With a little thoughtful effort, walking the dog can be beneficial and fun for both.

DOWN
Initially teach this command from the 'Sit' position. You can use the word 'Drop' or 'Down', but it is vital that your decide on one word only and stick to it.
- Have your dog sit on your left-hand side.
- Lower your hand, containing a treat, to directly in front of the dog's nose.
- Taking a small step forward, lower your hand to ground level. It may help to have your hand turned palm down so that the food is between your hand and the ground.

You will need to teach the "Down" with a treat used as a lure, and then progress to a verbal cue and a hand signal.

- Say "Drop", or "Down", as soon as the dog begins to go down in order to get the food.
- Give food as soon as the dog is lying down.
- Bring the dog back up to 'Sit' position and repeat a few more times.
- Repeat the full exercise for the next few days, gradually reducing the number of treats given to every third time or so.
- If the dog gets up into the 'Stand', rather than dropping 'Down', you are confusing the signals and probably have your hand too high. Be patient, check your action and wait for the pup to respond.

Another way to teach your Poodle to 'Down' is to have the dog sitting at your side, bring his outer leg forward while simultaneously pushing the dog gently away from his shoulder. As he goes on to his side say "Down". However, I find Poodles learn quickly using just signals and a treat.

STAY

Probably one of the most useful exercises you can teach the dog is to 'Stay', or 'Wait'. To begin with, this is best done in a quiet, relaxing atmosphere where there is very little distraction.

- Have your Poodle sit at your side in the 'Sit' position.
- Say the word "Stay" without using the dog's name. You can give a signal by using a flat hand in front of the dog's nose.
- Move forward one step with your right leg, then move back immediately before the dog has time to move. Give a treat.
- Repeat this four or five times.
- When the dog responds by staying on request you can progress by moving another step and turning to face the dog so that you are still fairly close.
- Do not lower your hand at this point otherwise your dog will think you are giving him the Come signal and he will move forward.
- Return to your position beside the dog and give a treat.
- Repeat a few more times.
- Gradually lengthen the distance and time that you move away from your Poodle before you return.
- If the dog comes out of the 'Stay', he needs the exercise to be reinforced, so go back to the beginning and start again. Don't chastise your dog for coming to you. Repeat the exercise from the beginning. Once the dog has got the idea

Build up the Stay exercise in easy stages.

PLAY RETRIEVE
The Poodle has a natural desire to retrieve.

The Poodle waits for his ball to be thrown.

Powering back with the ball.

Ready to give up the ball on request.

you can repeat doing a 'Down-Stay' and then a 'Stand-Stay'.

- Don't try to rush on to the next exercise. Give your dog time for the lesson to be learned. To begin with, only ask your dog to 'Stay' when you intend to walk away and return. Gradually teach the same principle with minor distractions, such as after a run in the playing field or at training classes, where he will learn to 'Sit and Stay' with other trained dogs for a couple of minutes. When he is proficient you can commence to 'Stay-Come'.

FETCH

Teaching a Poodle to fetch things is easy as he is a natural retriever and loves to carry things about in his mouth.

- Initially, throw an article like a ball, a pair of knotted socks, or a favourite play toy, a short distance in front of the pup at nose/eye level. Your Poodle will undoubtedly chase after it.
- Clap your hands and he will bring the article in his mouth, provided that the object is not too heavy to carry about.
- When the pup reaches you the reward is that you throw the object again. After a few repeats, end the game with a treat. Give the object back and play zigzag with it (not tug).
- The next stage is to try this in the garden. Again, the reward for fetching is that the game continues. It ends with praise or a food treat.

Articles that are brought to you to play with that you do not want the pup to have should be ignored, then taken away and replaced with the pup's toy. As the pup develops you can tell him to wait while you throw the object, then immediately throw your hand forward and say "Fetch". When the dog returns to you, offer him a treat at nose level in exchange for the item retrieved. Repeat the exercise, but stop before the pup gets tired or bored. You can soon ask your dog to sit in front of you, article still in mouth, then take the article, offering the treat as reward for retrieving.

ELEMENTARY SEEK TRAINING

The dog's terrific ability to scent can be used to find lost articles and people. Training in basic 'Seek' will benefit Poodles and their owners and provide interest and fun when walking.

- Use a personal item, such as a glove, to commence.
- Walk along in longish grass, scuffing your feet to leave a scent.
- After a few paces, drop your article (which may have a reward, such as a piece of fresh meat, inside) making sure that your Poodle is aware of the drop.
- Signal to the ground with your

With practice, you can train your Poodle to use his nose to seek out articles.

hand low, pointing to the track, towards the article, and say "Fetch… Seek".

- Once the dog has reached the article, reward him with the treat you have dropped with your article.
- Repeat the exercise.
- Do this each day for five days and your Poodle will have learned 'Seek Back'. Once the dog has mastered the idea of what is required, reinforce with treats every other or third time.
- The distance between dropping the article and sending the dog back can be lengthened once the dog has mastered the exercise. Also, vary the retrieving article to prevent the dog from getting into the habit of retrieving one item only, such as a ball. The exercise of 'Fetch' should be taught before 'Seek'.

PROBLEM BEHAVIOUR

These basic exercises with the young pup sound simple, and they are. It only takes a few minutes a day to run through a play lesson and your Poodle will benefit tremendously from this short time with you. It has to be said that very few people have Poodles with behaviour problems that they have not created themselves through lack of understanding. The Poodle temperament is in-built to please. He will try to please at any cost. If you over-indulge him without giving any training, then expect a rather sweet, but very unruly dog to live with. A little time and a bit of thought on your part will give you a dog that is a complete joy to live with. When problems arise they are usually due to a lack of understanding rather than intended neglect. Most unwanted behaviour is caused by lack of early socialisation, combined with sheer, simple boredom and lack of exercise.

All dogs are one of a pack. You are the 'alpha' leader of the pack so you must lead and not allow any dog to be the 'alpha' of the pack, over you. Within a family of dogs living in the house, one dog or bitch will take the alpha role over the others while still respecting you as their alpha leader, the supreme master. The dog leader of the pack becomes so because you afford him the most liberties. In other words you treat him as though he is the most special of the dogs. Problems can occur here when a new puppy is introduced to the household and you (quite naturally wanting him to feel

It is OK to indulge your Poodle as long as he understands his place in the family pack.

loved and wanted) afford him the most lavish attention and chastise the older dog for 'putting the pup in his place'. Eventually, if you continue on this line of over-indulgence to the youngster, the young dog will challenge the older one for leadership. It is therefore essential when bringing in a new recruit, to ensure that the puppy gets to know the pecking order by allowing the established dog to make take the appropriate action. This will prevent the onset of fighting later on. Poodles are not natural fighters, but if you don't lead the pack an argument may take place at some stage.

My own dogs are afforded a lot of privileges, such as sleeping on the bed in the morning and getting on the settees. However, their basic training has instilled in them that they are submissive to me, and if they ever decide to squabble between themselves one word from me stops it in seconds. They have never been hit in their lives.

I have to say the only time I have to watch for any sort of difference of opinion in my lot is when a bitch is coming in, or going out of, season. There is no doubt that some bitches suffer pre-menstrual tension. Luckily this only lasts up to a week and then hormones and tempers return to normal.

A bitch with a litter is a different concern altogether and must be protected and allowed total privacy until the pups are about three to four weeks of age.

A bored dog can swiftly become destructive.

She will then naturally allow others in the pack to associate with her pups.

BOREDOM
In today's world, many dogs are no longer allowed to be dogs. They are enclosed in small areas with fitted carpet rather than being free to roam. Some are never taken for walks and allowed to run free and let off steam.

They are fed high-protein, energy-boosting food that makes them even more in need of exercise. They live in busy households where parents are out at work all day. Children are now very often banned from taking the dog to the park to play with their friends. Dogs are forbidden their natural instinct to chew on bones to exercise their jaws and help pass the time away. They are frequently shut away when guests come. Is it any wonder they get bored or extremely excitable and neurotic?

Help is at hand for individual problems, but do try to ensure your Poodle has a task in life other than to be an adornment. He is less likely to get bored – and consequently destructive – when his mind and body are adequately exercised.

Spend time walking/running your Poodle. Train him. Regular work will establish not only good control, but will also keep the dog's mind busy. Socialise your Poodle with other dogs early on, as soon as he arrives with you, so

that he can play and make friends. This will teach him social skills. Allow him to be part of the family. Tell him not to jump up at the table when you are eating rather than shut him away. He will very soon learn not to interrupt your mealtime.

NOT COMING WHEN CALLED

At some time all dogs will ignore a call – they may be investigating a smell, or may want to continue playing with another dog, or they may be chasing a bird. The frustration caused to the owner by this 'deafness' in their dog will often trigger a reaction of punishment. If you chastise your

Poodle when he does come, you are teaching him that to come means hurt and pain.

It is essential to teach 'Come' in a restricted area where distractions are at a minimum. Reinforce with praise and treats until the habit is formed. Then progress to an area such as a park and go through the exercises from start to finish, ensuring the dog understands what is required. If your Poodle makes the odd mistake, don't be too disheartened. Just go back a step and continue training.

JUMPING UP

Owners teach dogs to jump up quite unintentionally most of the time. It is easy enough to do. When we get a puppy we want to cuddle him. We clap our hands to gain the pup's attention and he comes. We bend down for him to jump on to our knee. We all do it. As the dog grows he still wants this wonderful cuddle in your arms. You, however, become less keen – by now your Poodle may weigh 40 lbs (18 kgs) or more, and he may be dirty or wet while you have on your best clothes. The situation is not so cute now. If your Poodle has been encouraged to jump up he may take a little patience and time to break the habit. Here are two methods you can try to eliminate this problem:

• As the dog come towards you, lower your hands (preferably containing a treat) to the level of the dog's nose, never higher, say "Sit" and give food.
• Another way to try is to turn

A controlled greeting is acceptable, but make sure your Poodle does not learn to demand attention.

away from the dog as he approaches, ignore him and then give praise only when he has his four feet on the ground.

Poodles love to jump so it is wise to think about this when you first get your pup. If your Poodle is over-excitable, even though he has been well socialised, try lowering the protein level in his diet, and/or, join an agility club.

PULLING ON THE LEAD

Dogs that pull on the lead are inadvertently taught to do so by the person that walks them. Most uninitiated dog owners walk their dogs on a tight lead – which will teach the dog to pull. The dog must be encouraged to walk beside you on a loose lead. Leads are there as a safety measure rather than to actively control the dog. You must go back to basic training using treats and encouragement and teach the art of heeling beside you, both off and on the lead. Do this in a restricted area with little distraction, and then progress to a more demanding area.

Some dogs love to pull (if they didn't, they wouldn't pull sleds). The use of a head collar, which controls the dogs head rather like the halter we use for horses, is often used when walking several dogs together at one time, when they have no real pack leader to follow. However, good lead training will mean they are unnecessary. That said, it is true to say that elderly people with large dogs often feel safer when walking their dogs in a head collar.

It is easy for a Poodle to become focused on one member of the family.

THE 'ONE PERSON' DOG

It is easy to teach the dog to be a one-person dog when only one person does everything for him. You walk him, you feed him, you groom him, you train him and you make the rules. The dog becomes yours. This situation may not always be what is required in the family pet. The best way to establish a good relationship between the Poodle and his family is for all the family to take a share in the responsibility of taking care of the dog. Take turns to feed, take turns to groom, etc, and soon your Poodle will look to you all for love and attention and not be so single minded.

STEALING

Dogs that are used to being around the family rarely steal food (unless they are starving) because they are quickly taught by their owners not to jump up at meal times. If you feed the dog at the table you will encourage begging and stealing. The dog can be told to 'Down' or go to his bed while you are eating your meal.

Poodles can however, as can any dog, get into the habit of

If you have enjoyed training your Poodle, why not have a go at one of the canine sports?

taking anything they fancy, whether it is food, clothes or the children's toys. The word 'Leave' is a good word to teach. To teach the dog to 'Leave', place an object of desire in front of the dog and tell him to "Sit" and "Leave". Then give a treat for his having done so. The 'Leave' command is not threatening. It is merely a statement. Reward is given for response. If the dog has picked up an object he is not allowed, take the object, say "Leave" and give the dog an object he is allowed.

Poodles love to greet you when you come home with some form of gift. It may be your slippers, a toy, or something you didn't wish him to have. It is your job to make sure that valuables are put safely away. You cannot chastise a natural retriever for carrying objects in his mouth. Just be sure those objects are his, although it is true to say that most (though not all) Poodles will carry even a fluffy toy about and play with it without ever chewing it to bits.

Poodles that chew wood (e.g. the dining chairs) usually have a dietary problems, or worms. Unfortunately, this can become habit, so see to the problem without delay and use a strong anti-chew or lavender polish on the wood to make it taste unpleasant

NEW CHALLENGES
Being highly intelligent, eager to please and quick to learn, many owners find that their Poodle takes to training very well indeed.

If you and your dog enjoy basic training, there are a number of other activities you can become involved in to increase your skills and have fun. If you are interested in conformation, or 'showing', refer to Chapter 8.

CANINE GOOD CITIZEN
Very often a novice dog owner will start early training by participating in the Kennel Club's 'Good Citizen Award Scheme', designed to encourage dog owners to train their dogs to be a credit in society.

The tests include:
- Heeling on a lead at the owner's side
- Basic commands, such as 'Sit' and 'Down'
- Being handled/petted by a stranger
- Socialising with a friendly attitude among other people and dogs.

Children are encouraged to handle dogs to obtain a certificate of Canine Good Citizenship.

OBEDIENCE
Basic obedience is required from all of our dogs. Some handlers/owners become extremely keen and take training a step further in order to participate in Obedience competitions. In North America, Poodle breeders Blanch Saunders and Helene Whitehouse-Walker developed the first Obedience test for all breeds in the 1930s. Since then, Poodles have become a familiar sight in the Obedience ring at all levels, in many countries of the world. The

A first step to starting in Obedience is to attend training and socialisation classes.

various Kennel Clubs throughout the world lay down rules and regulations and many registered Obedience Clubs are pleased to take Poodles and their owners.

There are different levels of Obedience tests, depending on ability, and if you and your Poodle are motivated, there is no reason why you should not compete at the top level.

WORKING/HUNTING
The Poodle was a working, hunting, herding, scenting, retrieving, tracking dog of such sensitivity and gentleness it was said to surpass all other breeds in its capabilities. Perhaps his downfall, or drawback, was his coat, which needed considerable attention compared to the

shorthaired working dogs, or even the Spaniel or Setter. Today's Poodle still carries those original hunting genes. With no training at all these instincts give the Poodle his ability to locate game. Trained, the Poodle is as indispensable to a bird hunter as any working bird dog.

For many years the Poodle has been noted for his outstanding consummate nature, but today this accomplished breed still retains his eminent ability to work, given the opportunity. In many parts of the world the Poodle works in hunting tests. In particular Canada, USA, Australia and some of the Scandinavian countries seem to take an interest in retaining the inherent working ability of this versatile breed.

The Poodle shows great sensitivity and skill as a hunting dog.

AGILITY POODLES

This is a sport where all three varieties of Poodle can compete
as the classes are divided by size: small, medium and large.

Over the A-frame. The contact equipment is the same for all three size classes.

A Miniature shows off his speed over a jump.

When working as a hunter's dog, the Poodle locates the game for the hunter's gun. The dog is sent out to fetch the downed bird, which he then retrieves to the hunter whether the bird be on land or in water. All hunters have a dog. This is essential to ensure that all shot, sometimes crippled, birds are found and dealt with.

In the Hunt Test the purpose is to duplicate real hunting situations. Stationed guns shoot the birds and then the dogs must swim through decoys and reeds to retrieve their prey. The dog is required to stay with the handler in duck blinds, to get into and out of boats and to be able to run through heavy brush and up and down gullies. The dog relies on his senses of sight and smell to find his retrieve. In more advanced dogs, hand and whistle are used by the handlers to give commands. The purpose of the test is to provide a way to determine hunting ability in breeding stock, encourage owners to develop their dog's working abilities and to showcase impressive dog work for the interested public.

AGILITY

This is possibly the fastest growing sporting activity among the dog-owning public, and Poodle owners in particular. Agility done for fun is a worthwhile exercise for both dog and handler/owner. Poodles love it. After embarking on a course you may well get the bug and decide to take part in competitions, where the idea is for the dog to participate in a canine athletic test of skills.

As a breed, Poodles will learn easily and are quick on their feet considering their size. However, it is essential to allow a Standard Poodle to grow to full maturity (about 13 months of age) before any serious training. Before this time the dog is not physically and

103

Powering through the tunnel.

sometimes mentally, capable of sustaining the effort demanded. Bone damage can, and has, resulted from too much stress on joints, as well as the early onset of Arthritis. The best way is to keep to short bursts of training and lavish plenty of reward/encouragement and praise for response.

Agility began as an informal demonstration at the 1978 Crufts dog show in England. You may have seen displays at Crufts or at the Horse of the Year Show held in London. In Agility, the dog is required to complete a course of obstacles in a specific order, rather like a horse at a show-jumping event. The obstacle course includes contact obstacles, tunnels, hurdles, weave poles, pause obstacles and jumps, which includes a jump through a tyre.

- **Contact obstacles:** Contact obstacles have ramps for the dog to ascend and descend. Helpers are needed on each side of the ramp when the dog is learning to master the art of climbing up or coming down from obstacles such as the dog walk, A-frame, crossover, see-saw and swing bridge. The dog must not jump off the obstacle from too great a height as he may hurt himself and would lose points in competition.
- **Tunnels:** In the Agility course there are two types of tunnel. There is a curved, rigid tunnel, which is bent to block the light when the dog enters the tunnel. There is also a collapsed tunnel, which has a rigid entrance while the remainder of the tunnel is a collapsed cloth tube that the dog must travel through.
- **Jumps:** Equestrian event hurdles were the original inspiration for agility; jumps are different only in height and width, which are determined by the size of the dog and its standard of training.
- **Pause:** The pause may not be seen so much in competition now. This exercise demands good control. There are two common pause obstacles; one is a table and the other a box. The dog enters the pause obstacle and must execute the Down position for five seconds. This does not sound

A Standard Poodle clears a jump with ease.

long, but when one considers the speed and excitement that both dog and handler are experiencing, this pause requires tremendous mind and action adjustment.

- **Tyres:** Tyre jumps are suspended on a frame. The dog jumps through the tyre. The height can be adjusted as in the hurdles. This is a simple and fun exercise to do with your Poodle in the garden. Often when playing together my dogs will jump, following each other, through the tyre.

In Agility competition there is no predefined order or number of obstacles necessary in the course. However, at each event an established order of obstacles must be followed. In competition a maximum time is set for

qualification with points deducted for improper clearing of an obstacle. The winning score is based upon the fastest time with the fewest penalty points.

If you are interested in taking up Agility, there are clubs devoted to teaching Poodles the skills for this sport, but these may not be within your reach. Ask at your local dog club for contacts with people who are active in Agility within your travelling capacity. Most Obedience clubs now have an Agility contact.

All dogs participating in Agility must have a sound understanding of basic obedience. Also, a buckle-type collar and a six-foot lead for training purposes are required.

You will also need treats (your dog's favourite piece of liver, cheese, or whatever) in a doggy bag around your waist or in an easily accessible pocket. With agility training, positive reinforcement and an absolute minimum of correction are the main training methods used. It is essential not to exhaust the dog physically or mentally and to keep training on an interesting and happy course. Safety at all times is paramount. The point of participation in Agility at any level, is for the dog and owner – as a team – to have fun.

FLYBALL
Flyball sounds exhilarating and it is. This is a sport greatly enjoyed by dogs and their handlers. It is a team game – a relay race. The

FLYBALL POODLES

The Poodle loves to retrieve and has no problem keeping up with the fast and furious pace of Flyball.

DANCING WITH DOGS

The first annual Heelwork to Music competition was held in 1966. Since then many Poodle owners have been taking an interest in participating in this activity. The dancing is either 'Freestyle', or 'Heelwork to Music'. The routines are judged on style and presentation as well as content and accuracy. Every year at Crufts, many dog fanciers look forward to the many spectacular displays and demonstrations with Poodles showing their unique ability to turn a paw to music. One treasured partnership is between Tracy Ansell and her wonderful white Standard Poodle 'Spirit' (Somanic on a Mission for Chalkwell). Tracy and Spirit are now world famous for their breathtaking and entertaining dancing to music.

All Poodles can learn to do tricks. Some dogs just take longer than others. The most important thing is to be very patient. Start with simple demands, things your dog does naturally. Poodles stand on their hind legs at any given opportunity, so it is easy to teach them to do this to command. They learn quickly when given a reward immediately they respond to any command.

team, consisting of four pairs of dogs and handlers, competes against other teams for speed and precision. The dog jumps over a series of hurdles and goes to the Flyball box, where he trips a lever to release a ball. The dog catches the ball and returns it to his handler back over the line of hurdles. All this takes place against the clock. The fastest time wins.

Participation in Flyball requires athletic ability in both the dog and his handler, but it is not as demanding as Agility. Only a few obstacles are required for training purposes, but it is essential for the dog and handler to work as a team with other participants and enter into the spirit of team co-operation.

In team relay races the dog is not allowed to cross the start line until the preceding dog's nose crosses the finish line. Handlers are required to stay behind the line. Any dog missing a jump or failing to retrieve the ball to the handler must re-run the course. The height of the jumps is determined by setting them to 4 inches (10 cms) below the withers of the shortest dog in the team. The minimum jump is 8 inches (20 cms), the maximum 16 inches (40 cms). Width between the jumps is 24 inches (60 cms) and the uprights are not more than 36 inches (90 cms) high. The jumps are set 10 feet (3 metres) apart with the first one 6 feet (1.8 metres) from the start/finish line and the last jump 15 feet (4.5 metres) from the Flyball box.

SUMMING UP

Training the Poodle is best started at a young age, as with any other breed of dog. But the clever Poodle will learn quickly at any age. Training is on-going, a way of life, which involves reciprocal respect. Any Poodle will love to please its owner, so a happy Poodle will learn quickly to fulfil his owner's requirements when given appreciative respect for his fantastic qualities.

THE PERFECT POODLE

Chapter 7

Conformation exhibition is the most popular of all dog sports. It consists of a beauty contest where dogs are presented in a ring by handlers for a judge to assess and place in order of merit. The judge examines each dog in turn, looking for type (correct structure, sound movement, coat texture) and most importantly, an exceptional temperament (showing kindness and intelligence with a sparkle for a sense of the ridiculous). Without a truly loving and loyal temperament the Poodle is nothing, no matter how wonderfully he is constructed. Soundness in all departments, including eyes, teeth, feet, bones, muscles is rated as important to the essential sustaining of a breed's characteristics. For this reason a

Breed Standard, laid down by the Kennel Club of each country, is adhered to for each breed of dog. The judge will study the Breed Standard and learn it by heart, and will hopefully be a conscientious person who cares about where the breed came from, its function and its prosperity. It has to be said that not all judges are as good as we would wish, but on the whole, they are fairly good at their job. Personality does come in to judging dogs, as some judges favour one aspect above another. This may, or may not seem fair, but it is a fact that exhibitors must live with if they continue to show dogs. Only judges of repute, caring to retain the versatile excellence of the Poodle, will ensure the breed's quality and perfection.

THE BREED STANDARDS
The American Kennel Club

(AKC) and the Fédération Cynologique Internationale (FCI) have slight differences to the British Kennel Club Breed Standard. However, all varieties of Poodle show successfully throughout the world under the various Standards.

Responding to public concern about the health of pure-bred dogs, the KC has inserted the following introductory paragraph to all Breed Standards:

A Breed Standard is the guideline which describes the ideal characteristics, temperament and appearance of a breed and ensures that the breed is fit for function. Absolute soundness is essential. Breeders and judges should at all times be careful to avoid obvious conditions or exaggerations which would be detrimental in any way to the health, welfare or soundness

POODLE

Standard: This poodle is being presented in the Continental Lion trim.

Toy: Proud carriage is a feature of the breed.

Miniature: This variety retains the same well balanced proportions as the Standard.

of this breed. From time to time certain conditions or exaggerations may be considered to have the potential to affect dogs in some breeds adversely, and judges and breeders are requested to refer to the Kennel Club website for details of any such current issues. If a feature or quality is desirable it should only be present in the right measure.

A happy, gay-spirited dog, without a trace of shyness or sharpness.

GENERAL APPEARANCE

UK
Well balanced, elegant looking with very proud carriage.

AKC
That of a very active, intelligent and elegant-appearing dog, squarely built, well proportioned, moving soundly and carrying himself proudly.

The Poodle has what is known as 'attitude'. This means he is proud and elegant with an outgoing look. 'Poetry-in motion' sums up the Poodle well.

CHARACTERISTICS

UK
Distinguished by a special type of clip for show activity and by a type of coat which does not moult.

AKC
Properly clipped in the traditional fashion and carefully groomed, the Poodle has about him an air of distinction and dignity peculiar to himself.

In the UK the Poodle is no longer required to be trimmed in the traditional Lion or Continental trim at the age of 12 months. Many Champions still have their Puppy trim. In the US, the traditional trim must be adhered to once the Poodle comes of age.

TEMPERAMENT

UK
Gay-spirited and good-tempered.

AKC
Temperament: Carrying himself proudly, very active, intelligent, the Poodle has about him an air of distinction and dignity peculiar to himself. Major fault: shyness or sharpness.

A happy dog, willing and gregarious. There is no reasons or excuse to breed from atypical Poodles.

HEAD AND SKULL

UK
Long and fine with slight peak. Skull not broad, moderate stop. Foreface strong, well chiselled, not falling away under eyes; cheek bones and muscle flat. Lips tight-fitting. Chin well defined but not protruding. Head in proportion to size of dog.
Eyes: Almond-shaped, dark, not set too close together, full of fire and intelligence. Eye colour – see Colour Clause.
Ears: Leathers long and wide, set low, hanging close to face.
Mouth: Jaws strong with perfect, regular complete scissor bite, i.e. upper teeth closely overlapping lower teeth and set square to the jaws. A full set of 42 teeth is desirable.

AKC
Eyes: Very dark, oval in shape and set far enough apart and positioned to create an alert

The eyes are dark and almond-shaped with an alert, intelligent expression.

intelligent expression. Major fault: eyes round, protruding, large or very light.

Ears: Hanging close to the head, set at or slightly below eye level. The ear leather is long, wide and thickly feathered; however, the ear fringe should not be of excessive length.

Skull: Moderately rounded, with a slight but definite stop. Cheekbones and muscles flat. Length from occiput to stop about the same as length of muzzle.

Muzzle: Long, straight and fine, with slight chiseling under the eyes. Strong without lippiness. The chin definite enough to preclude snipiness. Major fault: lack of chin. Teeth: White, strong and with a scissors bite. Major fault: undershot, overshot, wry mouth.

It should never be forgotten that the Poodle should be capable of carrying a large bird in his mouth. The term "long, straight and fine" is therefore sometimes misinterpreted; from time to time we see dogs with too fine a head and little under-jaw winning in the show ring. This is not taking the origin of the breed seriously and should not be encouraged.

Neither should the Poodle be in any way thick and heavy in the skull. The ideal is an attractive, well-balanced head. The head, however, is only one part of the dog, so we need to look for elegance and balance in the Poodle as a whole.

NECK

UK
Well proportioned, of good length and strong to admit of the head being carried high and with dignity. Skin fitting tightly at the throat.

AKC
Neck well proportioned, strong and long enough to permit the head to be carried high and with dignity. Skin snug at throat. The neck rises from strong, smoothly muscled shoulders. Major fault: ewe neck.

The neck is required to be long enough to give grace and elegance to the Poodle's outline. The proportion of the dog is important. Good carriage, which is desired, comes from balance in all departments, which includes the neck in relation to the length of back.

FOREQUARTERS

UK
Well laid back shoulders, strong and muscular. Legs set straight from shoulders, well muscled.

AKC
Forequarters: Strong, smoothly muscled shoulders. The shoulder blade is well laid back and approximately the same length as the upper foreleg. Major fault: steep shoulder. *Forelegs*: Straight and parallel when viewed from the front.

Correct front assembly results in correct head carriage.

When viewed from the side the elbow is directly below the highest point of the shoulder. The pasterns are strong. Dewclaws may be removed.

The desired laid back shoulder is important to the strength and outline of the Poodle. An upright neck allows for a short neck, not of good proportion. It takes time for a judge to learn the art of knowing bone structure. Practice with an experienced person will help achieve this.

The upper arm can be too short and give the Poodle an incorrect gait. The front legs stand in a direct line from the shoulder. The feet face forward and should be neither turned in or out. Some of the larger Poodles may be a little unsettled in their front movement during growth.

Correct front assembly will result in a correct head carriage. The head being carried slightly forward and not on top of the wither as we see in some Poodles with incorrect angles.

BODY

UK
Chest deep and moderately wide. Ribs well sprung and rounded. Back short, strong, slightly hollowed; loins broad and muscular.

AKC
The topline is level, neither sloping nor roached, from the highest point of the shoulder blade to the base of the tail, with the exception of a slight hollow just behind the shoulder.
Body: Chest deep and moderately wide with well sprung ribs. The loin is short, broad and muscular.

Even in the smallest Poodle the body should never give the impression of being weak. The chest is deep and well sprung, to give the appearance of a dog that is agile and has substance. The prosternum should appear obvious. The slight hollow behind the wither must not be so deep as to allow for weakness. Equally, the roach back is undesirable. The body should have good muscular quality.

HINDQUARTERS

UK
Thighs well developed and muscular; well bent stifles, hocks well let down; hindlegs turning neither in nor out.

Even in the smallest Poodle, the body should never appear weak. Pictured is Ch. Vanitonia Gloria May: Top Toy 2006, Top Female 2007, winner of 20 CCs including Best of Breed at Crufts 2008.

AKC
The angulation of the hindquarters balances that of the forequarters. Hind legs straight and parallel when viewed from the rear. Muscular with width in the region of the stifles which are well bent; femur and tibia are about equal in length; hock to heel short and perpendicular to the ground.

The rear movement of the Poodle should be in harmony with the front, to allow for an easy-on-the-eye, balanced gait. The hindquarters should be angulated but not to such a degree to appear exaggerated. Exaggeration is a weakness. Any sized Poodle should be capable of running, jumping and showing off all his agility and strength. No Poodle is a weakling, no matter his size.

The back legs should be set looking straight ahead, and not turning inward or outward. The hock, being low, gives strength. Again, balance and good proportion is essential in any Poodle.

FEET

UK
Tight, proportionately small, oval in shape, turning neither in nor out, toes arched, pads thick and hard, well cushioned. Pasterns strong.

AKC
The (fore) feet are rather small, oval in shape with toes well arched and cushioned on thick firm pads. Nails short but not excessively shortened. The feet turn neither in nor out. Major fault: paper or splay foot. When standing, the rear toes are only slightly behind the point of the rump. Major fault: cow-hocks.

Always an important feature, weak feet give rise to weakness elsewhere. We are looking for fairly small and neat, oval-shaped feet, which are well arched with thick pads that are well cushioned. These allow the Poodle his spring-like performance.

TAIL

UK

Previously customarily docked. *Docked*: Set on rather high, carried at slight angle away from the body, never curled or carried over back, thick at root. Undocked: Thick at root, set on rather high, carried away from the body and as straight as possible.

AKC

Tail straight, set on high and carried up, docked of sufficient length to insure a balanced outline.
Major fault: set low, curled, or carried over the back.

In many countries, the tail is no longer permitted to be docked. In the UK we have soon got used to this and most people now love their Poodles with tails. The tail should, however, still be carried away from the body at the base. The fashion for the American higher-set tail does allow for the undocked tail to be carried incorrectly in a tight curl over the back. At the time of writing, the tail may still be docked in the US.

We are now accustomed to Poodles with undocked tails.

GAIT/MOVEMENT

UK

Sound, free and light movement essential with plenty of drive.

AKC

A straightforward trot with light springy action and strong hindquarters drive. Head and tail carried up. Sound effortless movement is essential.

We are looking for balance, that light, springy action that flows forward with ease, without jolting up and down in a rise and fall. The gait should not reach too far forward or be stilted and short.

COAT

UK

Very profuse and dense; of good harsh texture. All short hair close, thick and curly. It is strongly recommended that the traditional lion clip be adhered to.

AKC

a) Quality: (1) Curly: of naturally harsh texture, dense throughout. (2) Corded: hanging in tight even cords of varying length; longer on mane or body coat, head, and ears; shorter on puffs, bracelets, and pompons.

(b) Clip: A Poodle under 12 months may be shown in the "Puppy" clip. In all regular classes, Poodles 12 months or over must be shown in the "English Saddle" or "Continental" clip. In the Stud Dog and Brood Bitch classes and in a non-competitive Parade of Champions, Poodles may be shown in the "Sporting" clip. A Poodle shown in any other type of clip shall be disqualified.

(1) "Puppy": A Poodle under a year old may be shown in the "Puppy" clip with the coat long. The face, throat, feet and base of the tail are shaved. The entire shaven foot is visible. There is a pompon on the end of the tail. In order to give a neat appearance and a smooth unbroken line, shaping of the coat is permissible.

(2) "English Saddle": In the "English Saddle" clip the face, throat, feet, forelegs and base of the tail are shaved, leaving puffs on the forelegs and a pompon on the end of the tail. The hindquarters are covered with a short blanket of hair

The coat should be profuse, with a good, harsh texture.

except for a curved shaved area on each flank and two shaved bands on each hindleg. The entire shaven foot and a portion of the shaven leg above the puff are visible. The rest of the body is left in full coat but may be shaped in order to insure overall balance.

(3) "Continental": In the "Continental" clip, the face, throat, feet, and base of the tail are shaved. The hindquarters are shaved with pompons (optional) on the hips. The legs are shaved, leaving bracelets on the hindlegs and puffs on the forelegs. There is a pompon on the end of the tail. The entire shaven foot and a portion of the shaven foreleg above the puff are visible. The rest of the body is left in full coat but may be shaped in order to insure overall balance.

(4) "Sporting": In the "Sporting" clip, a Poodle shall be shown with face, feet, throat, and base of tail shaved, leaving a scissored cap on the top of the head and a pompon on the end of the tail. The rest of the body, and legs are clipped or scissored to follow the outline of the dog leaving a short blanket of coat no longer than one inch in length. The hair on the legs may be slightly longer than that on the body.

The range of colours is a feature of the breed.

In all clips the hair of the topknot may be left free or held in place by elastic bands. The hair is only of sufficient length to present a smooth outline. "Topknot" refers only to hair on the skull, from stop to occiput. This is the only area where elastic bands may be used.

The Poodle's wool coat has texture. The adult coat will feel quite harsh when not conditioned or sprayed to keep it from drying out and tangling. It will, however, curl within moments of being brushed, unless it has been recently bathed. Even then, using blow driers some Poodle coats will be full of waves. This is natural and shows a good coat. For the perfection of scissoring the coat needs to be dried as straight as possible.

COLOUR

UK

All solid colours. White and creams to have black nose, lips and eye rims, black toenails desirable. Browns to have dark amber eyes, dark liver nose, lips, eye rims and toenails. Apricots and reds to have dark eyes with black points or deep amber eyes with liver points. Blacks, silvers and blues to have black nose, lips, eye rims and toenails. Creams, apricots, reds, browns, silvers and blues may show varying shades of the same colour up to 18 months. Clear colours preferred.

AKC

The coat is an even and solid color at the skin. In blues, grays, silvers, browns, cafe-au-laits, apricots and creams the coat may show varying shades of the same color. This is frequently present in the somewhat darker feathering of the ears and in the tipping of the ruff. While clear colors are definitely preferred, such natural variation in the shading of the coat is not to be considered a fault. Brown and cafe-au-lait Poodles have liver-colored noses, eye-rims and lips, dark toenails and dark amber eyes. Black, blue, gray, silver, cream and white Poodles have black noses, eye-rims and lips, black or self colored toenails and very dark eyes. In the apricots while the foregoing coloring is preferred, liver-colored noses, eye-rims and lips, and amber eyes are permitted but are not desirable. Major fault: color of nose, lips and eye-rims incomplete, or of

117

wrong color for color of dog. Parti-colored dogs shall be disqualified. The coat of a parti-colored dog is not an even solid color at the skin but is of two or more colors.

While the UK Breed Standard states that the Poodle's coat should be one solid colour at 18 months, anyone who breeds Poodles knows that this is virtually impossible. The US version shows more realism. Having had silver and blue Poodles for 40 years, I know that at all times Poodles of a solid colour show various shades of that colour for their entire lives. Most breed judges understand this. However, the variation in the coat can cause confusion. The shading is in no way a Poodle of two or more colours – which is not desired according to the Breed Standard.

SIZE

UK
Poodles (Standard): Over 38 cms (15 ins).

Most Standards are larger than the lower size stipulated in the Breed Standard.

Poodles (Miniature): Height at shoulder should be under 38 cms (15 ins) but not under 28 cms (11 ins).
Poodles (Toy): Height at shoulder should be under 28 cms (11 ins).

AKC
The Standard Poodle is over 15 inches (38 cms) at the highest point of the shoulders. Any Poodle which is 15 inches or less in height shall be disqualified from competition as a Standard Poodle.

The Miniature Poodle is 15 inches or under at the highest point of the shoulders, with a minimum height in excess of 10 inches (25 cms). Any Poodle which is over 15 inches or is 10 inches or less at the highest point of the shoulders shall be disqualified from competition as a Miniature Poodle.

The Toy Poodle is 10 inches or under at the highest point of the shoulders. Any Poodle which is more than 10 inches at the highest point of the shoulders shall be disqualified from competition as a Toy Poodle.

As long as the Toy Poodle is definitely a Toy Poodle, and the Miniature Poodle a Miniature Poodle, both in balance and proportion for the Variety, diminutiveness shall be the deciding factor when all other points are equal.

It is important that the Toy (left) and the Miniature (right) remain as distinct varieties.

Proportion: To insure the desirable squarely built appearance, the length of body measured from the breastbone to the point of the rump approximates the height from the highest point of the shoulders to the ground. Substance: Bone and muscle of both forelegs and hindlegs are in proportion to size of dog.

The large Poodle is more than 15 inches (38 cm) at the shoulder, according to the Breed Standard. It is rare indeed to find a true standard Poodle so small. A miniature Poodle may grow over the desired height of 15 inches, but he is still a miniature, as a toy Poodle growing over the desired height of 11 inches is still a toy Poodle.

In 2007, the Kennel Club decided that miniature and toy Poodles need no longer be measured in the show ring. However, the Poodle council in coalition with the breed clubs continue to insist their judges measure. This is to prevent the miniature and toy poodles blending into one size.

FAULTS

UK

Any departure from the foregoing points should be considered a fault and the seriousness with which the fault should be regarded should be in exact proportion to its degree and its effect upon the health and welfare of the dog.
Note: **Male animals should have two apparently normal testicles fully descended into the** scrotum. (Last Updated 2009, Interim.)

AKC

Major Faults: **Any distinct deviation from the desired characteristics described in the Breed Standard.**
Disqualifications: **Size: A dog over or under the height limits specified shall be disqualified. Clip: A dog in any type of clip other than those listed under coat shall be disqualified. Parti-colors: The coat of a parti-colored dog is not an even solid color at the skin but of two or more colors. Parti-colored dogs shall be disqualified.**

VALUE OF POINTS (AKC)
• **General appearance, temperament, carriage and condition 30**

Judges need to bear in mind the original working function of the breed.

- Head, expression, ears, eyes and teeth 20
- Body, neck, legs, feet and tail 20
- Gait 20
- Coat, color and texture 10

(Approved August 14, 1984, Reformatted March 27, 1990, With thanks to the American Poodle Club)

INTERPRETING THE BREED STANDARD

We have seen that originally the Poodle was bred from selected stock to do the job of retrieving ducks from land and water, hunting and other activities. Poodles were found to be faithful and devoted companions. If judges as well as breeders remember this, the Poodle will be in safe hands. His future as a special dog with the ability to perform to a high standard in a wide range of activities, will be secure.

It is sometimes a worry that the quest of some judges is to want the finest Poodles imaginable. Yes, the Breed Standard calls for fine heads, but exaggerated, skinny heads, lacking in depth of foreface, will change the face and the intelligence of the Poodle. Does the winning Poodle have a back skull with adequate width to ensure what scientists have always agreed upon – that the Poodle appears to have the most brain room of any dog? Does he have a foreface with enough strength to carry a duck (relatively fine behind the eyes, relatively strong in front)? If he fails in this important department the judge is not doing a very good job in considering origin, preservation, and future, of this fantastic breed. Those imagining the Toy Poodle is any different are not very aware. The Toy Poodle, as tiny as he may appear at 11 inches (27.5 cms) or less, is a dog packed with spirit, full of character, and perfectly capable of galloping beside a horse, jumping in competition, executing obedience exercises, and holding himself proud in society. I hope they are never bred to be what their name implies, a toy.

Heaviness is not something to be encouraged, although it has to be said that this is seen less than the over-willowy Poodle. The

Poodle has a deep chest, is athletic, very stylish, with a fairly light structure that gives him the ability to move with great speed and enables him to sustain incredible endurance.

THE SHOW SCENE

In many countries around the world Poodle people show their dogs in the conformation show ring. Many countries have their own popular show – the World Show on the Continent, Sydney Royal in Australia, Westminster in North America. In Britain we have Crufts. Probably every non-dog-owning person, as well as those who own dogs, has heard of Crufts. Certainly, for a large percentage of dog enthusiasts Crufts is a show that is held as the most famous, most glamorous and most distinguished dog show in the world. For the dog showing fraternity in Britain, Crufts is a show that holds singular respect. Everyone who shows a dog in conformation wants to qualify for Crufts. In 2009 Crufts drew an entry of more than 25,000 dogs over the four days. People come from all over the world to visit and exhibit at this show.

Anyone, young, old, disabled or able-bodied can show dogs, although it has to be said that in top competition, a very high

Showing your Poodle at Championship level is highly competitive.

standard of handling ability will help a good dog win over other good dogs. Basically, people show dogs in conformation to win. We also do it for fun, and for the social aspect of interaction with other Poodle people.

This interest has resulted in Poodle Clubs forming, some for individual sizes of Poodle, all over the world. The Poodle Club UK dates back to 1886.

TYPES OF SHOW

There are many different types of show held all over this country and abroad. In all countries shows are run under the

governing Kennel Club's rules and regulations, with the exception of fun pet shows.

UK SHOWS

• **Companion show:** These are classed as fun events in Britain and attract a good many pet owners and novice exhibitors wishing to practice their handling skills. However, today's Companion show does attract the more seasoned campaigner who wishes to use the friendly, non-pressurised show as a training ground for their young potentially winning stock.

Most Companion shows are run in aid of charity or a good cause and are therefore sponsored by local shops, as well as some of the large pet food manufacturers. Prizes, such as dog biscuits, often exceed those received from more prestigious shows, but although a good place for socialising and having fun there is little or no status gained from wins, however many they amount to.

• **Match meetings:** These are run by local canine societies or by a breed club. Dogs are judged on a knockout system of competition, involving two dogs competing against each other at a time. Champions,

Show presentation in the USA is of the highest calibre.

popular, attracting the largest show entries. On offer at most Championship shows are the elusive Challenge Certificates, for the best dog and best bitch of the day. General canine societies and breed clubs run Championship shows.

SHOWS IN THE USA

- **Matches:** These are organised by speciality clubs and breed clubs. Champions are ineligible for entry.
- **Specialty Championship shows:** These are organised by a Breed club. They attract attract large entries and include a sweepstakes class, which has a different judge to the other classes. Judges must be qualified to judge at this level. Points are on offer, which go towards a Champion title.
- **All Breed Championship shows:** As in the UK, all breeds are scheduled and have specialist judges. Entries are large. Points are on offer, which go towards the Champion title. To become a Champion in the USA, a dog must win 15 points. The system there makes it far easier for a dog to gain a title than in the UK.

FCI RULES

There are more than 100 countries that come under the umbrella of the FCI. Many countries have small and large All Breed and Breed shows. Where a title is on offer, a dog can start competing for certificates from the age of nine months. The certificate is

Reserve CC winners and Junior Warrant winners are ineligible. These matches are terrific grounding for young puppies and prove invaluable for novice handlers. They are also a useful ground for judges to learn their art.
- **Open shows:** General breed societies as well as individual breed clubs run Open shows. These shows are open to all, but titles and status are not gained. General breed Open

shows include usually 3-6 classes for each breed scheduled. Breed clubs often run a 16 class Open show for their breed. Entries at general Open shows are usually minimal, while the breed club Open show usually attracts a vast number of enthusiasts.
- **Championship shows:** These are the largest shows where Poodle entries often exceed 100, although at this time the Standard Poodle is the more

awarded in a Winner's Class, which the dog has to qualify to enter on the day. This class is not open to Champions. In the Winner's Class, the judge can hand out several (or no) awards of Champion quality. If the winning dog gets this award, he is also awarded a certificate.

To become a Champion under FCI rules, a Poodle has to win three certificates under at least two different judges, and at least one of the certificates after the age of 24 months.

All dogs with the award Champion Quality, including Champions and Veterans, go on to the Best of Sex competition. At International shows, the CACIB (International Certificate) is awarded in this class.

To become an International Champion, a Poodle must win four CACIBs under at least three different judges, with at least one year between the first and the last CACIB, and in at least three countries, one of which has to be the owner's home country or the breed's country of origin. For Poodles two CACIBs are awarded in each sex; one for blacks, browns and whites, and one for silver and apricots. The dog can start competing for CACIBs from the age of 15 months. Before becoming an International Champion, he has to be a National Champion.

There are minor differences between some countries, so before judging abroad one must study the rules of the country concerned.

A Standard Poodle Champion made up under FCI rules.

GETTING STARTED

Most people start their initiation into the show world with a puppy and continue it through until the dog has either gained a title, or such time as the owner feels the dog has achieved all he is going to. Sometimes a new exhibitor will get the hang of showing and then get themselves a better quality dog to try to gain more credit in the show ring.

It is advisable to attend local ring training classes to gain experience and learn correct ring procedure, as well as giving the puppy time to become proficient at performing in crowded halls where many other dogs are noisily attending. It would be pointless to take an unprepared Poodle to a show, put him in the ring and expect him to behave. All show Poodles, as with all working/competing Poodles, must be trained to do the job required. They do not learn these skills by luck. Good handlers

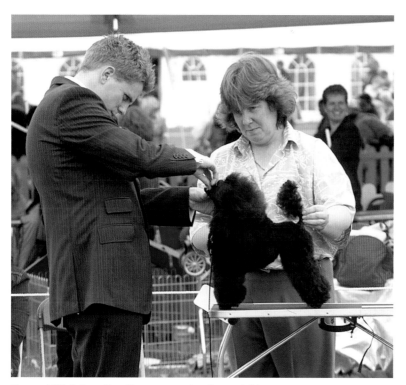

Toy and Miniature Poodles are examined on a table.

spend a lot of time and lavish love and devotion on their protégés to get a top performance from them.

The Miniature and Toy Poodle must learn to stand close to the edge of a table while being handled by the judge. He will also need to become accustomed to having the 'measure' put over him to confirm his size. All Poodles in the show ring must stand still while the judge 'goes over' them. They must also move in straight lines away from and back to the judge, and move in circles and triangles at heel with their handler. The dog must behave in the company of other dogs and people. For this reason show ring classes are a must: to socialise the Poodle, get him used to strangers examining him so that he does not back off from the judge, and so that he will perform happily with an outgoing personality

Training at classes should begin as soon as possible. Teach the Stand as described in Chapter 6, giving treats as reward. Accustom your Poodle to stand on your left-hand side. Ask somebody who knows the dog to stroke him while he stands still. With a young pup don't take too long doing this or he will move out of frustration. Reward the correct response with a treat. Once the dog is happy with this, ask somebody the dog doesn't know as well to stroke him while he is in the stand. Offer a treat while this takes place. I advocate that it is far better to have a doggy person who handles confidently to do this, because they have a different attitude to those who haven't any idea what they are supposed to be doing. This gives the dog a head start as he feels the relaxed confidence of the pretend judge's approach. Repeat over a course of weeks, giving a treat for reward when the dog has stood still for a few moments and allowed the pretend judge to stroke him from head to toe. Progress to repeating the exercise at ring training classes on a regular basis.

We have already achieved the 'heel' in our early puppy training (see Chapter 6). Now practise trotting away from your pretend judge with dog at heel, then back again. Perform a circle and a triangle with progression.

All Poodles should become acclimatised to standing on a table to be groomed. Once accustomed to the table and quite happy to stand still, ask your pretend judge to stroke the dog from head to foot. If the pup has finished teething, your judge can lift the dog's lips to gently look at his teeth. Miniature and Toy Poodles can now learn to be measured on a table. It is useful to have your own measure and show it to the dog a few times, allowing him to sniff, then give a treat. Place the measure over the

HAPPY AND HEALTHY

Chapter 8

Poodles in their three sizes (distinguished by adult shoulder height) are dogs with a good life span that can run well into double figures, provided their needs are met. The Poodle is renowned as a faithful companion and a willing friend on a non-conditional basis. He will, however, of necessity rely on you for food and shelter, accident prevention and medication. A healthy Poodle is a happy chap.

The nature of the Poodle's coat is a major feature of the breed. Left to its own devices without clipping and grooming, it will felt into a matt against the skin. Regular attention to the coat is therefore vital. Poodles shed little or no hair, making them a popular choice for those with an allergy to dog fur. There are some significant genetic conditions which have been recognised in the Poodle. They will be covered in depth later in the chapter.

ROUTINE HEALTH CARE

VACCINATION

There is much debate over the issue of vaccination at the moment. The timing of the final part of the initial vaccination course for a puppy and the frequency of subsequent booster vaccinations are both under scrutiny. Some manufacturers have licensed vaccines against certain diseases for use every three years, after the initial course. An evaluation of the relative risk for each disease plays a part, depending on the local situation.

Many owners think that the actual vaccination is the protection, so that their puppy can go out for walks as soon as he or she has had the final part of the puppy vaccination course.

This is not the case. The rationale behind vaccination is to stimulate the immune system into producing protective antibodies, which will be triggered if the patient is subsequently exposed to that particular disease. This means that a further one or two weeks will have to pass before an effective level of protection will have developed.

Vaccines against viruses stimulate longer-lasting protection than those against bacteria, whose effect may only persist for a matter of months in some cases. There is also the possibility of an individual failing to mount a full immune response to a vaccination: although the vaccine schedule may have been followed as recommended, that particular dog remains vulnerable.

As in human medicine, adverse reactions to vaccination can occur, albeit rarely, and must be weighed against the advantages of

Puppies need protection from a number of major contagious diseases.

protection against serious, sometimes potentially life-threatening, diseases.

A dog's level of protection against rabies, as demonstrated by the antibody titre in a blood sample, is routinely tested in the UK in order to fulfil the requirements of the Pet Travel Scheme (PETS). This is not required at the current time with any other individual diseases in order to gauge the need for booster vaccination or to determine the effect of a course of vaccines; instead, your veterinary surgeon will advise a protocol based upon the vaccines available, local disease prevalence, and the lifestyle of you and your dog.

It is worth remembering that maintaining a fully effective level of immune protection against the disease appropriate to your locale is vital: these are serious diseases, which may result in the death of your dog, and some may have the potential to be passed on to his human family (so-called zoonotic potential for transmission). This is where you will be grateful for your veterinary surgeon's own knowledge and advice.

The American Animal Hospital Association laid down guidance at the end of 2006 for the vaccination of dogs in North America. Core diseases were defined as distemper, adenovirus, parvovirus and rabies. So-called non-core diseases are kennel cough, Lyme disease and leptospirosis. A decision to vaccinate against one or more non-core diseases will be based on an individual's level of risk, determined on lifestyle and where you live in the US.

Do remember, however, that the booster visit to the veterinary surgery is not 'just' for a booster. I am regularly correcting my clients when they announce that they have 'just' brought their pet for a booster. Instead, this appointment is a chance for a full health check and evaluation of how a particular dog is doing. After all, we are all conversant with the adage that a human year is equivalent to seven canine years.

There have been attempts in recent times to reset the scale for two reasons: small breeds live longer than giant breeds, and dogs are living longer than previously. I have seen dogs of 17 and 18 years of age, but to say a dog is 119 or 126 years old is plainly meaningless. It does emphasise the fact, though, that a dog's health can change dramatically over the course of a single year, because dogs age at a far faster rate than humans.

For me as a veterinary surgeon, the booster vaccination visit is a challenge: how much can I find of which the owner was unaware, such as rotten teeth or a heart murmur? Even monitoring bodyweight year upon year is of use, because bodyweight can creep up, or down, without an owner realising. Being overweight is unhealthy, but it may take an outsider's remark to make an owner realise that there is a problem. Conversely, a drop in bodyweight may be the only pointer to an underlying problem.

The diseases against which dogs are vaccinated include:

ADENOVIRUS

Canine adenovirus 1 (CAV-1) affects the liver (hepatitis) and is seen within affected dogs as the classic 'blue eye', while CAV-2 is a cause of kennel cough (see later). Vaccines often include both canine adenoviruses.

DISTEMPER

This disease is sometimes called 'hardpad' from the characteristic changes to the pads of the paws. It has a worldwide distribution, but fortunately vaccination has been very effective at reducing its occurrence. It is caused by a virus and affects the respiratory, gastro-intestinal (gut) and nervous systems, so it causes a wide range of illnesses. Fox and urban stray dog populations are most at risk and are usually responsible for local outbreaks.

KENNEL COUGH

Also known as infectious tracheobronchitis, *Bordetella bronchiseptica* is not only a major cause of kennel cough but also a common secondary infection on top of another cause. Being a bacterium, it is susceptible to treatment with appropriate antibiotics, but the immunity stimulated by the vaccine is therefore short-lived (six to 12 months).

This vaccine is often in a form to be administered down the nostrils in order to stimulate local immunity at the point of entry, so to speak. Do not be alarmed

Poodles are a relatively healthy breed, but it is a good idea for your dog to have a routine check-up.

to see your veterinary surgeon using a needle and syringe to draw up the vaccine, because the needle will be replaced with a special plastic introducer, allowing the vaccine to be gently instilled into each nostril. Dogs generally resent being held more than the actual intra-nasal vaccine, and I have learnt that covering the patient's eyes helps greatly.

Kennel cough is, however, rather a catch-all term for any cough spreading within a dog population – not just in kennels, but also between dogs at a training session or breed show, or even mixing in the park. Many of these infections may not be *B.*

bronchiseptica but other viruses, for which one can only treat symptomatically. Parainfluenza virus is often included in a vaccine programme, as it is a common viral cause of kennel cough.

Kennel cough can seem alarming. There is a persistent cough accompanied by the production of white frothy spittle, which can last for a matter of weeks; during this time the patient is highly infectious to other dogs. I remember when it ran through our five Border Collies – there were white patches of froth on the floor wherever you looked! Other features include sneezing, a

Kennel cough can spread rapidly among dogs that live together.

runny nose, and eyes sore with conjunctivitis. Fortunately, these infections are generally self-limiting, most dogs recovering without any long-lasting problems, but an elderly dog may be knocked sideways by it, akin to the effects of a common cold on a frail, elderly person.

LEPTOSPIROSIS

This disease is caused by *Leptospira interogans*, a spiral-shaped bacterium. There are several natural variants or serovars. Each is characteristically found in one or more particular host animal species, which then acts as a reservoir, intermittently shedding leptospires in the urine. Infection can also be picked up at mating, via bite wounds, across the placenta, or through eating the carcases of infected animals (such as rats).

A serovar will cause actual clinical disease in an individual when two conditions are fulfilled:

the individual is not the natural host species, and is also not immune to that particular serovar.

Leptospirosis is a zoonotic disease, known as Weil's disease in humans, with implications for all those in contact with an affected dog. It is also commonly called rat jaundice, reflecting the rat's important role as a carrier. The UK National Rodent Survey 2003 found a wild brown rat population of 60 million, equivalent at the time to one rat per person. Wherever you live in the UK, rats are endemic, which means that there is as much a risk to the Poodle living with a family in a town as the Poodle leading a more rural lifestyle.

Signs of illness reflect the organs affected by a particular serovar. In humans, there may be a flu-like illness or a more serious, often life-threatening disorder involving major body organs. The illness in a susceptible dog may be mild, the

dog recovering within two to three weeks without treatment but going on to develop long-term liver or kidney disease. In contrast, peracute illness may result in a rapid deterioration and death following an initial malaise and fever. There may also be anorexia, vomiting, diarrhoea, abdominal pain, joint pain, increased thirst and urination rate, jaundice, and ocular changes. Haemorrhage is also a common feature, manifesting as bleeding under the skin, nosebleeds, and the presence of blood in the urine and faeces.

Treatment requires rigorous intravenous fluid therapy to support the kidneys. Being a bacterial infection, it is possible to treat leptospirosis with specific antibiotics, although a prolonged course of several weeks is needed. Strict hygiene and barrier nursing are required in order to avoid onward transmission of the disease.

Vaccination reduces the severity of disease, but cannot prevent the dog becoming a carrier.

The situation in America is less clear-cut. Blanket vaccination against leptospirosis is not considered necessary, because it only occurs in certain areas. There has also been a shift in the serovars implicated in clinical disease, reflecting the effectiveness of vaccination and the migration of wildlife reservoirs carrying different serovars from rural areas, so you must be guided by your veterinarian's knowledge of the local situation.

LYME DISEASE

This is a bacterial infection transmitted by hard ticks. It is restricted to those specific areas of the US where ticks are found, such as the north-eastern states, some southern states, California and the upper Mississippi region. It does also occur in the UK, but at a low level, so vaccination is not routinely offered.

Clinical disease is manifested primarily as limping due to arthritis, but other organs affected include the heart, kidneys and nervous system. It is readily treatable with appropriate antibiotics, once diagnosed, but the causal bacterium, *Borrelia burgdorferi,* is not cleared from the body totally and will persist.

Prevention requires both vaccination and tick control, especially as there are other diseases transmitted by ticks. Ticks carrying *B. burgdorferi* will transmit it to humans as well, but an infected dog cannot pass it to a human.

Fortunately the incidence of Lyme disease is rare in the UK.

PARVOVIRUS (CPV)

Canine parvovirus disease first appeared in the late 1970s, when it was feared that the UK's dog population would be decimated by it because of the lack of immunity in the general canine population. While this was a terrifying possibility at the time, fortunately it did not happen.

There are two forms of the virus (CPV-1, CPV-2) affecting domesticated dogs. It is highly contagious, picked up via the mouth/nose from infected faeces.

The incubation period is about five days. CPV-2 causes two types of illness: gastro-enteritis and heart disease in puppies born to unvaccinated dams, both of which often result in death. Infection of puppies under three weeks of age with CPV-1 manifests as diarrhoea, vomiting, difficulty breathing, and fading puppy syndrome. CPV-1 can cause abortion and foetal abnormalities in breeding bitches.

Occurrence is mainly low now, thanks to vaccination, although a recent outbreak in my area did claim the lives of several puppies and dogs. It is also occasionally seen in the elderly unvaccinated dog.

RABIES

This is another zoonotic disease and there are very strict control measures in place. Vaccines were once available in the UK only on an individual basis for dogs being taken abroad. Pets travelling into the UK had to serve six months' compulsory quarantine so that any pet incubating rabies would be identified before release back into the general population. Under the Pet Travel Scheme (PETS), provided certain criteria are met (check the DEFRA website for up-to-date information) then dogs can re-enter the UK without being quarantined.

Dogs to be imported into the US have to show that they were vaccinated against rabies at least 30 days previously; otherwise, they have to serve effective internal quarantine for 30 days from the date of vaccination against rabies, in order to ensure they are not incubating rabies. The exception is dogs entering from countries recognised as being rabies-free, in which case it has to be proved that they lived in that country for at least six months beforehand.

Most puppies will carry a burden of roundworm. This is a Standard Poodle puppy pictured with a Toy Poodle puppy.

PARASITES

A parasite is defined as an organism deriving benefit on a one-way basis from another, the host. It goes without saying that it is not to the parasite's advantage to harm the host to such an extent that the benefit is lost, especially if it results in the death of the host. This means a dog could harbour parasites, internal and/or external, without there being any signs apparent to the owner. Many canine parasites can, however, transfer to humans with variable consequences, so routine preventative treatment is advised against particular parasites.

Just as with vaccination, risk assessment plays a part – for example, there is no need for routine heartworm treatment in the UK (at present), but it is vital in the US and in Mediterranean countries.

ROUNDWORMS (NEMATODES)

These are the spaghetti-like worms that you may have seen passed in faeces or brought up in vomit. Most of the deworming treatments in use today cause the adults roundworms to disintegrate, thankfully, so that treating puppies in particular is not as unpleasant as it used to be!

Most puppies will have a worm burden, mainly of a particular roundworm species (*Toxocara canis*), which reactivates within the dam's tissues during pregnancy and passes to the foetuses developing in the womb. It is therefore important to treat the dam both during and after pregnancy, as well as the puppies.

Professional advice is to continue worming every one to three months. There are roundworm eggs in the environment and, unless you examine your dog's faeces under a microscope on a very regular basis for the presence of roundworm eggs, you will be unaware of your dog having picked up roundworms, unless he should have such a heavy burden that he passes the adults.

It takes a few weeks from the time that a dog swallows a *Toxocara canis* roundworm egg to himself passing viable eggs (the pre-patent period). These eggs are not immediately infective to other animals, requiring a period of maturation in the environment, which is primarily temperature-dependent and therefore shorter in the summer (as little as two weeks) than in the winter. The eggs can survive in the environment for two years and more.

There are deworming products that are active all the time, which will provide continuous protection when administered as often as directed. Otherwise, treating every month will, in effect, cut in before a dog could theoretically become a source of roundworm eggs to the general population.

It is the risk to human health that is so important: *T. canis* roundworms will migrate within our tissues and cause all manner of problems, not least of which (but fortunately rarely) is blindness. If a dog has roundworms, the eggs also find their way on to his coat where they can be picked up during stroking. Sensible hygiene is therefore important. You should always carefully pick up your dog's faeces and dispose of them appropriately, thereby preventing the maturation of any eggs present in the fresh faeces.

TAPEWORMS (CESTODES)

When considering the general dog population, the primary source of the commonest tapeworm species will be fleas, which can carry the eggs. Most multi-wormers will be active against these tapeworms. They are not a threat to human health, but it is unpleasant to see the wriggly ricegrain tapeworm segments emerging from your dog's back passage while he is lying in front of the fire, and usually when you have guests for dinner!

A tapeworm of significance to human health is *Echinococcus granulosus*, found in a few parts of the UK, mainly in Wales. Man is an intermediate host for this tapeworm, along with sheep, cattle and pigs. Inadvertent ingestion of eggs passed in the faeces of an infected dog is followed by the development of so-called hydatid cysts in major organs, such as the lungs and liver, necessitating surgical removal. Dogs become infected

through eating raw meat containing hydatid cysts. Cooking will kill hydatid cysts, so avoid feeding raw meat and offal in areas of high risk.

There are specific requirements for treatment with praziquantel within 24 to 48 hours of return into the UK under the PETS. This is to prevent the inadvertent introduction of *Echinococcus multilocularis*, a tapeworm carried by foxes on mainland Europe, which is transmissible to humans, causing serious or even fatal liver disease.

HEARTWORM (DIROFILARIA IMMITIS)

Heartworm infection has been diagnosed in dogs all over the world. There are two prerequisites: the presence of mosquitoes, and a warm, humid climate.

When a female mosquito bites an infected animal, it acquires *D. immitis* in its circulating form, as microfilariae. A warm environmental temperature is

needed for these microfilariae to develop into the infective third-stage larvae (L3) within the mosquitoes, the so-called intermediate host. L3 larvae are then transmitted by the mosquito when it next bites a dog. Therefore, while heartworm infection is found in all parts of the United States, it is at differing levels. An occurrence in Alaska, for example, is probably a reflection of a visiting dog having previously picked up the infection elsewhere.

Heartworm infection is not currently a problem in the UK, except for those dogs contracting it while abroad without suitable preventative treatment. Global warming and its effect on the UK's climate, however, could change that.

It is a potentially life-threatening condition, with dogs of all breeds and ages being susceptible without preventative treatment. The larvae can grow to 14 inches within the right side of the heart, causing primarily signs

Currently heartworm is not a problem in the UK.

of heart failure and ultimately liver and kidney damage. It can be treated but prevention is a better plan. In the US, regular blood tests for the presence of infection are advised, coupled with appropriate preventative measures, so I would advise liaison with your veterinary surgeon.

For dogs travelling to heartworm-endemic areas of the EU, such as the Mediterranean coast, preventative treatment should be started before leaving the UK and maintained during the visit. Again, this is best arranged with your veterinary surgeon.

MITES

There are five types of mite that can affect dogs:

i) **Demodex canis**: This mite is a normal inhabitant of canine hair follicles, passed from the bitch to her pups as they suckle. The development of actual skin disease or demodicosis depends on the individual. It is seen frequently around the time of puberty and after a bitch's first season, associated with hormonal changes. There may, however, be an inherited weakness in an individual's immune system, enabling multiplication of the mite.

The localised form consists of areas of fur loss without itchiness, generally around the face and on the forelimbs, and 90 per cent will recover without treatment. The other 10 per cent develop the juvenile-onset generalised form, of which half will recover spontaneously. The other half may be depressed, go off their food, and show signs of itchiness due to secondary bacterial skin infections.

Treatment is often prolonged over several months and consists of regular bathing with a specific miticidal shampoo, often clipping away fur to improve access to the skin, together with a suitable antibiotic by mouth. There is also now a licensed 'spot-on' preparation available. Progress is monitored by the examination of deep skin scrapings for the presence of the mite; the initial diagnosis is based upon abnormally high numbers of the mite, often with live individuals being seen.

Some Poodles may develop demodicosis for the first time in middle-age (more than four years of age). This often reflects underlying immunosuppression by an internal disease, so it is important to identify such a cause and correct it where possible, as well as treating the skin condition.

(ii) **Sarcoptes scabei**: This mite characteristically causes an intense pruritus or itchiness in the affected Poodle, causing him to incessantly scratch and bite at himself, leading to marked fur

The Poodle's dense, profuse coat means that preventative treatment against external parasites is essential.

loss and skin trauma. Initially starting on the elbows, earflaps and hocks, without treatment the skin on the rest of the body can become affected, with thickening and pigmentation of the skin. Secondary bacterial infections are common.

Unlike *Demodex*, this mite lives at the skin surface, and it can be hard to find in skin scrapings. It is therefore not unusual to treat a patient for sarcoptic mange (scabies) based on the appearance of the problem even with negative skin scraping findings, and especially if there is a history of contact with foxes, which are a frequent source of the scabies mite.

It will spread between dogs and can therefore also be found in situations where large numbers of dogs from different backgrounds are mixing together. It will cause itchiness in human, although the mite cannot complete its life cycle on us, so treating all affected dogs should be sufficient. Fortunately, there is now a highly effective 'spot-on' treatment for *Sarcoptes scabei*.

(iii) *Cheyletiella yasguri*: This fur mite is the most common to affect dogs. It is often called 'walking dandruff' because it can be possible to see collections of the small white mite moving about over the skin surface. There is excessive scale and dandruff formation, and mild itchiness. It is be transmissible to humans, causing a pruritic rash.

Diagnosis is by microscopic examination of skin scrapings,

FLEAS

There are several species of flea, which are not host-specific. A dog can be carrying cat and human fleas as well as dog fleas, but the same flea treatment will kill and/or control them all. It is also accepted that environmental control is a vital part of a flea control programme. This is because the adult flea is only on the animal for as long as it takes to have a blood meal and to breed; the remainder of the life cycle occurs in the house, car, caravan, shed...

There is a vast array of flea control products available, with various routes of administration: collar, powder, spray, 'spot-on', or oral. Flea control needs to be applied to all pets in the house, regardless of whether they leave the house, since fleas can be introduced into the home by other pets and their human owners. Discuss your specific flea control needs with your veterinary surgeon.

coat combings and sticky tape impressions from the skin and fur. Treatment is with an appropriate insecticide, as advised by your veterinary surgeon.

(iv) *Otodectes cynotis*: A highly transmissible otitis externa (outer ear infection) results from the presence in the outer ear canal of this ear mite, characterised by exuberant production of dark earwax. The patient will frequently shake his head and rub at the ear(s) affected. The mites can also spread on to the skin adjacent to the opening of the external ear canal, and may transfer elsewhere, such as to the paws.

When using an otoscope to examine the outer ear canal, the heat from the light source will often cause any ear mites present to start moving around. I often offer owners the chance to have a look, because it really is quite an extraordinary sight! It is also possible to identify the mite from earwax smeared on to a slide and examined under a microscope.

Cats are a common source of ear mites. It is not unusual to find ear mites during the routine examination of puppies and kittens. Treatment options include specific eardrops acting against both the mite and any secondary infections present in the auditory canal, and certain 'spot-on' formulations. It is vital to treat all dogs and cats in the household to prevent recycling of the mite between individuals.

(v) (Neo-) *Trombicula autumnalis*: The free-living mite or harvest mite can cause an

Ticks now occur nationwide in the UK.

intense local irritation on the skin. Its larvae are picked up from undergrowth, so they are characteristically found as a bright orange patch on the web of skin between the digits of the paws. It feeds on skin cells before dropping off to complete its life cycle in the environment.

Its name is a little misleading, because it is not restricted to the autumn nor to harvest-time; I find it on the earflaps of cats from late June onwards, depending on the prevailing weather. It will also bite humans.

Treatment depends on identifying and avoiding hotspots for picking up harvest mites, if possible. Checking the skin, especially the paws, after exercise and mechanically removing any mites found will reduce the chances of irritation, which can be treated symptomatically. Insecticides can also be applied – be guided by your veterinary surgeon.

TICKS

Ticks have become an increasing problem in recent years throughout Britain. Their physical presence causes irritation, but it is their potential to spread disease that causes concern. A tick will transmit any infection previously contracted while feeding on an animal: for example *Borrelia burgdorferi,* the causal agent of Lyme disease (see page 131).

The life cycle of the tick is curious: each life stage takes a year to develop and move on to the next. Long grass is a major habitat. The vibration of animals moving through the grass will stimulate the larva, nymph or adult to climb up a blade of grass and wave its legs in the air as it 'quests' for a host on to which to latch for its next blood meal. Humans are as likely to be hosts, so ramblers and orienteers are advised to cover their legs when going through rough long grass.

Removing a tick is simple – provided your dog will stay still. The important rule is to twist gently so that the tick is persuaded to let go with its mouthparts. Grasp the body of the tick as near to your dog's skin as possible, either between thumb and fingers or with a specific tick-removing instrument, and then rotate in one direction until the tick comes away. I keep a plastic tick hook in my wallet at all times.

A-Z OF COMMON AILMENTS

ANAL SACS, IMPACTED

The anal sacs lie on either side of the anus at approximately four and eight o'clock, if compared with the face of a clock. They fill with a particularly pungent fluid, which is emptied on to the faeces as they move past the sacs to exit from the anus. Theories abound as to why these sacs should become impacted periodically and seemingly more so in some dogs than others.

The irritation of impacted anal sacs is often seen as 'scooting', when the backside is dragged along the ground. Some dogs will also gnaw at their back feet or over the rump.

Increasing the fibre content of the diet helps some dogs; in others, there is underlying skin disease. It may be a one-off occurrence for no apparent reason. Sometimes an infection can become established, requiring antibiotic therapy, which may need to be coupled with flushing out the infected sac under sedation or general anaesthesia. More rarely, a dog will present with an apparently acute-onset anal sac abscess, which is incredibly painful.

DIARRHOEA
Cause and treatment much as Gastritis (see below).

EAR INFECTIONS
The dog has a long external ear canal, initially vertical then horizontal, leading to the eardrum, which protects the middle ear. If your Poodle is shaking his head, then his ears will need to be inspected with an auroscope by a veterinary surgeon in order to identify any cause, and to ensure the eardrum is intact. A sample may be taken from the canal to be examined under the microscope and

The long drop ears of the Poodle can be prone to ear infections.

cultured, to identify causal agents before prescribing appropriate eardrops containing antibiotic, antifungal agent and/or steroid. Predisposing causes of otitis externa or infection in the external ear canal include:

- Presence of a foreign body, such as a grass awn
- Ear mites, which are intensely irritating to the dog and stimulate the production of brown wax, predisposing to infection
- Previous infections, causing the canal's lining to thicken, narrowing the canal and reducing ventilation
- Swimming – the Poodle is thought to have been originally

bred as a gundog to retrieve water fowl so many Poodles will swim, but water trapped in the external ear canal can lead to infection, especially if the water is not clean. Likewise, care is also needed when bathing your Poodle.

FOREIGN BODIES
Internal: Items swallowed in haste without checking whether they will be digested can cause problems if they lodge in the stomach or obstruct the intestines, necessitating surgical removal. Acute vomiting is the main indication. Common objects I have seen removed include stones from the garden, peach

The Poodle is naturally agile, but watch out for stiffness after exercise.

stones, babies' dummies, golf balls, and, once, a lady's bra…

It is possible to diagnose a dog with an intestinal obstruction across a waiting room from a particularly 'tucked-up' stance and pained facial expression. These patients bounce back from surgery dramatically. A previously docile and compliant obstructed patient will return for a post-operative check-up and literally bounce into the consulting room.

External: Grass awns are adept at finding their way into orifices such as a nostril, down an ear, and into the soft skin between two digits (toes), whence they start a one-way journey due to the direction of their whiskers. In particular, I remember a grass awn that migrated from a hindpaw, causing abscesses along the way but not yielding itself up until it erupted through the skin in the groin!

GASTRITIS

This is usually a simple stomach upset, most commonly in response to dietary indiscretion. Scavenging constitutes a change in the diet as much as an abrupt switch in the food being fed by the owner

There are also some specific infections causing more severe gastritis/enteritis, which will require treatment from a veterinary surgeon (see also Canine Parvovirus under 'Vaccination' on page 131).

Generally, a day without food, followed by a few days of small, frequent meals of a bland diet (such as cooked chicken or fish), or an appropriate prescription diet, should allow the stomach to settle. It is vital to ensure the patient is drinking and retaining sufficient water to cover losses resulting from the stomach upset in addition to the normal losses to be expected when healthy. Oral rehydration fluid may not be very appetising for the patient, in which case cooled boiled water should be offered. Fluids should initially be offered in small but frequent amounts to avoid over-drinking, which can result in further vomiting and thereby dehydration and electrolyte imbalances. It is also important to wean the patient back on to routine food gradually or else another bout of gastritis may occur.

JOINT PROBLEMS

It is not unusual for older Poodles to be stiff after exercise, particularly in cold weather. This is not really surprising, given that they are such busy dogs when young. Your veterinary surgeon will be able to advise you on ways of helping your dog cope with stiffness, not least of which will be to ensure that he is not overweight. Arthritic joints do not need to be burdened with extra bodyweight!

LUMPS

Regularly handling and stroking your dog will enable the early detection of lumps and bumps. These may be due to infection (abscess), bruising, multiplication of particular cells from within the body, or even an external parasite (tick). If you are worried about any lump you find, have it checked by a veterinary surgeon.

OBESITY

Being overweight does predispose to many other problems, such as diabetes mellitus, heart disease and joint problems. It is so easily prevented by simply acting as your Poodle's conscience. Ignore pleading eyes and feed according to your dog's waistline. The body condition is what matters qualitatively, alongside monitoring that individual's bodyweight as a quantitative measure. The Poodle should, in my opinion as a health professional, have at least a suggestion of a waist and it should be possible to feel the ribs beneath only a slight layer of fat.

Neutering does not automatically mean that your Poodle will be overweight. Having an ovario-hysterectomy does slow down the body's rate of working, castration to a lesser extent, but it therefore means that your dog needs less food. I recommend cutting back a little on the amount of food fed a few weeks before neutering to accustom your Poodle to less food. If she looks a little underweight on the morning of the operation, it will help the

A dog that is kept fit and lean will live a longer, healthier life.

veterinary surgeon as well as giving her a little leeway weight-wise afterwards. It is always harder to lose weight after neutering than before, because of this slowing in the body's inherent metabolic rate.

TEETH

Eating food starts with the canine teeth gripping and killing prey in the wild, incisor teeth biting off pieces of food and the molar teeth chewing it. To be able to eat is vital for life, yet the actual health of the teeth is often overlooked: unhealthy teeth can predispose to disease, and not just by reducing the ability to eat.

The presence of infection within the mouth can lead to bacteria entering the bloodstream and then filtering out at major organs, with the potential for serious consequences. That is not to forget that simply having dental pain can affect a dog's wellbeing, as anyone who has had toothache will confirm.

Veterinary dentistry has made huge leaps in recent years, so that it no longer consists of extraction as the treatment of necessity. Good dental health lies in the hands of the owner, starting from the moment the dog comes into your care. Just as we have taken on responsibility for feeding, so

There is a difference in the inherited conditions that can affect the Standard Poodle and the two smaller varieties.

we have acquired the task of maintaining good dental and oral hygiene. In an ideal world, we should brush our dogs' teeth as regularly as our own, but the Poodle puppy who finds having his teeth brushed is a huge game and excuse to roll over and over on the ground requires loads of patience, twice a day.

There are alternative strategies, ranging from dental chewsticks to specially formulated foods, but the main thing is to be aware of your dog's mouth. At least train your puppy to permit full examination of his teeth. This will not only ensure you are checking in his mouth regularly but will also make your veterinary surgeon's job easier when there is a real need for your dog to 'open wide!'

INHERITED DISORDERS

Any individual, dog or human, may have an inherited disorder by virtue of the genes acquired from the parents. This is significant not only for the health of that individual but also because of the potential for transmitting the disorder on to that individual's offspring and to subsequent generations, depending on the mode of inheritance.

There are control schemes in place for some inherited disorders. In the US, for example, the Canine Eye Registration Foundation (CERF) was set up by dog breeders concerned about heritable eye disease, and provides a database of dogs who have been examined by diplomates of the American

College of Veterinary Ophthalmologists.

As well as screening programmes, it is now possible to directly identify the genes responsible for certain inherited disorders. This means that, by running DNA tests before breeding, individuals carrying unwanted genes can be identified and breeding programmes designed accordingly. All that is required is a blood sample and/or a cheek swab, depending on the condition being assessed, procedures which are generally well tolerated.

There are many conditions which seem to be particularly prevalent in the Poodle but may reflect popularity of the Poodle breeds within the canine population in general, or the physical characteristics of the Poodle. Many are often described as a breed predisposition, for example:

- Diabetes mellitus (sugar diabetes)
- Gastric dilatation-volvulus ('bloat') in Standard Poodles
- Haemorrhagic gastroenteritis in Toy and Miniature Poodles
- Hyperadrenocorticism or Cushing's disease
- Insulinoma in Standard Poodles (a rare tumour of the pancreas)
- Primary hypoparathyrodism in Miniature Poodles

To date, a number of conditions have been confirmed in the Poodle as being hereditary. In general, there is some variation between conditions inherited in the Standard Poodle compared with those inherited in the Miniature and Toy Poodles. In alphabetical order, these include:

CORNEAL DYSTROPHY

The cornea is the transparent layer across the front of the eye. Corneal dystrophy is an inherited, non-inflammatory disorder affecting both eyes which manifests as opacities (often round or oval or doughnut-shaped) within the cornea. Progression is generally slow in the Poodle and may or may not lead to blindness. It is generally not painful, unless an ulcer develops.

A congenital form occurring in young Poodle puppies less than ten weeks old is usually a transient feature.

CRYPTORCHIDISM

(Miniature and Toy Poodles) During fetal development, the testicles form high within the abdomen and migrate down through the abdomen, out along the inguinal canal and into their final position in the scrotum. A dog is said to be cryptorchid if one or both testicles is absent from the scrotum and is instead located within the inguinal canal or within the abdomen. In the Miniature and Toy Poodles, this is thought to be inherited in an autosomal recessive fashion.

ENTROPION

This is an inrolling of the eyelids, most often affecting the medial lower eyelids. There are degrees of entropion, ranging from a slight inrolling to the more

EPILEPSY
(Miniature and Toy Poodles)

Inheritance is suspected. This is often called juvenile epilepsy because it manifests in the immature and young adult Poodle (six months to three years old), with convulsions occurring singly or in clusters.

It is very alarming as an owner to see your dog having a fit because you feel utterly helpless. It is vital to note when a fit or cluster of fits occurs on a calendar or in a diary, together with information about concurrent happenings (for example, family gathering, television switched on, fireworks, middle of the night).

Even if a young adult Poodle came to see me having had just one fit, I would be unlikely to start medication at once because 'every dog is allowed one or two fits'. Once medication has started, then one may never know whether or not he would have had any more fits at all. If it is needed to control the fits then medication will, from the nature of the problem, be life-long.

There are also reports of Narcolepsy-cataplexy in Miniature and Standard Poodles similar to the condition in humans. It is thought to be inherited, and generally manifests before the age of one year.

serious case, requiring surgical correction because of the pain and damage to the surface of the eyeball (CERF).

GENERALISED PROGRESSIVE RETINAL ATROPHY (GPRA)

(Miniature and Toy Poodles) As the name indicates, there is gradual widespread degeneration of the retina's light-detecting rods and cones at the back of the eye, usually affecting night vision first. The rate of progression is variable: the end result is often a loss of vision and blindness,

although some dogs may retain some vision. There is often associated cataract formation. GPRA starts to become apparent in the mature dog between two to eight years age, but can be detected with an ophthalmoscope by three to five years of age. Rigorous screening is vital under Schedule A of the *BVA/KC/ISDS Scheme in the UK, CERF in the US.

GPRA is inherited as an autosomal recessive, and carriers can now be identified with a DNA test (from The Animal

HAEMOPHILIA A

Haemophilia is the most common disorder of blood coagulation in humans and animals, inherited in a sex-linked recessive fashion. This means that the male is either affected or clear, whilst females can alternatively be carriers for the trait. Haemophilia A arises from a deficiency of blood clotting Factor VIII.

There are many ways in which haemophilia A can manifest, at worst as sudden death. There may be early indications, such as prolonged bleeding when the baby teeth are lost or unexpected bruising under the skin. A problem may not become apparent until after surgery such as routine neutering or an injury. Treatment will often require a blood transfusion.

Health Trust, Newmarket in the UK) to ensure they are only bred with clear individuals.

HEREDITARY CATARACT (HC)
Standard Poodle: This is not a congenital condition. There is progressive development of cataracts starting at the equator of the lens in both eyes, commonly quoted as starting at one year old and culminating in blindness by two years of age. It is controlled under Schedule A of the *BVA/KC/ISDS Eye Scheme.
Miniature and Toy Poodles: In these Poodles, the cataracts develops in a different pattern from that in the Standard Poodle and from an older age, generally four to five years old, and causing visual impairment. Inheritance is suspected.

HIP DYSPLASIA
This is an inherited orthopaedic disorder which shows a spectrum of changes, and can be crippling. There is instability of the malformed hip joints, such that arthritis develops in an attempt to achieve better stability but may simply contribute to or worsen the level of pain. The degree of change seen radiographically is not necessarily a good guide to the effect on the individual: a dog with a very high hip score may not be as lame as a dog with a lower one, hence the need for a standardised scoring/grading system. Any breed can be screened for Hip dysplasia under the **BVA/KC schemes in the UK. It is advised for the Standard Poodle by the Kennel Club's Accredited Breeder Scheme but not currently for Miniature and Toy Poodles. As of 1st November 2007, the hips of 535 Standard Poodles had been scored, with a mean total score of

14 although with a very wide range of 0 - 74, the worst possible total score being 106 and the best zero. Only a relatively small number of Miniature Poodles (33) had had their hips scored, giving the same mean total score but with a marginally better range of 4-58.

HYPOADRENOCORTICISM (ADDISON'S DISEASE)
(Standard Poodle)
Under-production of hormones by the adrenal glands has wide-ranging effects within the body. Clinical signs can be very vague, such as vomiting, lethargy and poor appetite. An Addisonian crisis may be precipitated by stress, or when blood potassium rises to such a level that the sodium/potassium balance affects heart function, leading to heart failure and death. A genetic predisposition is suspected from the occurrence in certain family lines of Standard Poodle, manifesting in young or middle-aged individuals.

HYPOTHYROIDISM
This is a common endocrine problem in the canine population. Some sources consider it to be inherited in the Poodle where it commonly arises from autoimmune thyroiditis (the body's immune system mounts an attack on its own thyroid gland).

Clinical signs are variable and it can be hard to definitively diagnose. In some cases, a response to trial thyroid hormone supplementation may be needed to confirm the diagnosis. A dog with hypothyroidism may be overweight despite a normal appetite and resistant to weight-control measures, he may have coat and skin changes, or simply be lethargic.

IMMUNE-MEDIATED THROMBOCYTOPAENIA

This arises from destruction of the blood platelets by the body's immune system at a rate faster than their production by the bone marrow. The platelets play an important role in blood clotting so effects include nosebleeds, bruising under the skin, weakness and lethargy, blood in urine/faeces. This is more common in the Poodle than would be expected compared with the general dog population so inheritance is suspected.

LEGGE-CALVE-PERTHES DISEASE

(Miniature and Toy Poodles)
Also called Legge-Perthes disease, the problem is more accurately described as an avascular necrosis of the femoral head, meaning the ball of the thigh bone dies, resulting in severe pain and lameness. Surgery can be quite effective. Early diagnosis and treatment through pain relief and resting of the affected back-leg in a sling may avoid the need for surgical intervention.

LYSOSOMAL STORAGE DISEASES

There are several forms which result in neurological signs in

It is advised that Standard Poodles are screened for hip dysplasia.

puppies between the ages of three and twelve months, depending on the particular disease. Fortunately they are rare. Inheritance is suspected.

MITRAL VALVE DISEASE

(Miniature Poodle)
This is a common form of heart disease in old dogs more than ten years old, but the early development of mitral valve disease has been recognised in the Miniature Poodle, and to a lesser extent in the Toy and Standard Poodles. A characteristic heart murmur is an early sign. Once diagnosed, medical therapy can help support the ailing heart.

OPTIC NERVE HYPOPLASIA

(Miniature and Toy Poodles)
This is a congenital condition, present from birth. The optic nerve has failed to develop so that the affected eye's pupil fails to respond to light and the individual is blind in that eye. Inheritance is suspected. It can be hard to distinguish on ophthalmoscopic examination from micropapilla (small optic disc) which occurs rarely in the Miniature and Toy Poodles as another congenital condition which does not, however, affect eyesight.

PATELLAR LUXATION

(Miniature and Toy Poodles)
This is the condition that I point out to my children when I spot a dog walking along the road, giving a little hop for a few steps every now and again. The kneecap or patella is slipping out

of position, locking the knee or stifle so that it will not bend, causing the characteristic hopping steps until the patella slips back into its position over the stifle joint. Surgical correction is possible in severely affected dogs, but many simply carry on intermittently hopping, the long-term effect inevitably being arthritis of the stifle.

PATENT DUCTUS ARTERIOSUS
(Miniature and Toy Poodles)
This is a common congenital abnormality which may be inherited in these two Poodle types. The ductus arteriosus is a normal feature of the fetus, running from the pulmonary artery to the descending aorta and enabling most of the blood to bypass the lungs during life in the womb; the lungs are not needed for respiration but simply need enough blood for their own development. With the pup's first breath, and by the eighth day of life, this shunt should seal and no longer be patent so that all the blood leaving the right side of the heart is taken to the lungs and thence back to the left side of the heart.

Persistence of the ductus arteriosus adversely affects the cardiovascular system and will ultimately result in heart failure. The characteristic continuous heart murmur may also be felt with the fingers across the chest wall as a so-called 'thrill'. Early diagnosis is essential before clinical signs have developed, enabling surgical intervention in most, but not all, cases.

Owners are becoming increasingly aware of the benefits of complementary therapies. Swimming or hydrotherapy is an excellent way of providing stress-free exercise.

RENAL DISEASE, JUVENILE
(Standard Poodle)
Affected individuals develop kidney failure from a few months of age, with increase urination and thirst, urine leakage, weight loss and difficulty house-training. The mode of inheritance has not been identified.

SEBACEOUS ADENITIS (SA)
(Standard Poodle)
Sebaceous adenitis is a skin disease in which the sebaceous glands becoming inflamed. Eventually, the glands may be completely destroyed leading to progressive loss of hair.

Signs include excessive dandruff, greasy or dry scaling, skin darker in colour, a musty odour, thickening of the skin and hair loss ranging from scattered to total baldness. In the Standard Poodle, the scaling is often silvery. In severely affected animals, secondary skin infections may occur.

There is no cure for SA, but it can be treated. Frequent baths and oil treatments have been found helpful in removing scale and lubricating the skin. Antibiotics are used to treat secondary infections.

In Poodles, testing has shown SA to be inherited as a simple autosomal recessive trait. Diagnosis can be made by biopsy.

VON WILLEBRAND'S DISEASE
This inherited bleeding disorder manifests in the affected individual as a tendency to bleed easily, and should be suspected if there is prolonged bleeding after an injury or surgery, if there is bleeding from the nose/gums, or if blood is seen in the urine. Affected individuals can lead normal lives, but special care must be taken to avoid inadvertent injuries around the house by applying padding to sharp corners, and when clipping the coat and claws, for example. It can be diagnosed with blood tests, and DNA testing is available.

*British Veterinary Association/Kennel Club/International Sheep Dog Society
** British Veterinary Association/Kennel Club

COMPLEMENTARY THERAPIES
Just as for human health, I do believe that there is a place for alternative therapies alongside and complementing orthodox treatment under the supervision

of a veterinary surgeon. That is why 'complementary therapies' is a better name.

Because animals do not have a choice, there are measures in place to safeguard their wellbeing and welfare. All manipulative treatment must be under the direction of a veterinary surgeon who has examined the patient and diagnosed the condition that he or she feels needs that form of treatment. This covers physiotherapy, chiropractic, osteopathy and swimming therapy. For example, dogs with arthritis who cannot exercise as freely as they were accustomed will enjoy the sensation of controlled non-weight-bearing exercise in water, and will benefit with improved muscling and overall fitness.

All other complementary therapies such as acupuncture, homoeopathy and aromatherapy, can only be carried out by veterinary surgeons who have been trained in that particular field. Acupuncture is mainly used in dogs for pain relief, often to good effect. The needles look more alarming to the owner, but they are very fine and are well tolerated by most canine patients. Speaking personally, superficial needling is not unpleasant and does help with pain relief. Homoeopathy has had a mixed press in recent years. It is based on the concept of treating like with like. Additionally, a homoeopathic remedy is said to become more powerful the more it is diluted.

Remember, you are responsible for your Poodle's health and wellbeing for the duration of his life.

SUMMARY

As the owner of a Poodle, you are responsible for his care and health. Not only must you make decisions on his behalf, you are also responsible for establishing a lifestyle for him that will ensure he leads a long and happy life. Diet plays as important a part in this, as does exercise.

For the domestic dog, it is only in recent years that the need has been recognised for changing the diet to suit the dog as he grows, matures and then enters his twilight years. So-called life-stage diets try to match the nutritional needs of the dog as he progresses through life.

An adult dog food will suit the Poodle living a standard family life. There are also foods for those Poodles tactfully termed as obese-prone, such as those who have been neutered or are less active than others, or simply like their food. Do remember, though, that ultimately you are in control of your Poodle's diet, unless he is able to profit from scavenging!

On the other hand, prescription diets are of necessity fed under the supervision of a veterinary surgeon because each is formulated to meet the very specific needs of particular health conditions. Should a prescription diet be fed to a healthy dog, or to a dog with a different illness, there could be adverse effects.

It is important to remember that your Poodle has no choice. As his owner, you are responsible for any decision made, so it must be as informed a decision as possible. Always speak to your veterinary surgeon if you have any worries about your Poodle. He is not just a dog; from the moment you brought him home, he became a member of the family.

THE AUTHORS

EILEEN GEESON (JANAVONS)

Eileen Geeson has been actively involved with Poodles since about the age of twelve and has bred English, Swedish, Finnish and International Champions.

Eileen became a Championship judge of all three sizes of Poodle in 1985, and at the British Utility Breeds Association in 1986 attracted a world record entry of Standard Poodles. She also judges most of the Utility Group Breeds.

Eileen has also competed in Obedience and Agility and has worked with Pets as Therapy with Standard Poodles.

Eileen writes 'Points To Ponder', a weekly column for *Dog World* and has written about Poodles in numerous publications.

She lives in Lincolnshire with her husband, Roy, and their five Standard Poodles, which include her two latest winning puppies Janavons Sea Dancer and Janavons Here Comes Holly.

ALISON LOGAN MA VetMB MRCVS

Alison qualified as a veterinary surgeon from Cambridge University in 1989, having been brought up surrounded by all manner of animals and birds in the north Essex countryside. She has been in practice in her home town ever since, living with her husband, two children and Labrador Retriever Pippin.

She contributes on a regular basis to *Veterinary Times, Veterinary Nurse Times, Dogs Today, Cat World* and *Pet Patter,* the PetPlan newsletter. In 1995, Alison won the Univet Literary Award with an article on Cushing's Disease, and she won it again (as the Vetoquinol Literary Award) in 2002, writing about common conditions in the Shar-Pei.

See Chapter Eight: Happy and Healthy.

USEFUL ADDRESSES

BREED CLUBS

To obtain up-to-date contact information for the following breed clubs, please contact the Kennel Club:
- British Toy Poodle Club
- Eastern Counties Poodle Club
- International Poodle Club
- London & Home Counties Toy Poodle Club
- Mercia Toy Poodle Association
- Midland Counties Poodle Club
- Miniature Poodle Club
- North Western Poodle Club
- Northern Toy Poodle Club
- Northumbria Poodle Club
- Poodle Club
- Poodle Club of Scotland
- Poodle Club of Wales
- South Western Poodle Club
- Standard Poodle Club
- Trent to Tweed Poodle Club

KENNEL CLUBS

American Kennel Club (AKC)
5580 Centerview Drive
Raleigh, NC 27606
Telephone: 919 233 9767
Fax: 919 233 3627
Email: info@akc.org
Web: www.akc.org

The Kennel Club (UK)
1 Clarges Street
London, W1J 8AB
Telephone: 0870 606 6750
Fax: 0207 518 1058
Web: www.the-kennel-club.org.uk

TRAINING AND BEHAVIOUR

Association of Pet Dog Trainers
PO Box 17, Kempsford, GL7 4WZ
Telephone: 01285 810811
Email: APDToffice@aol.com
Web: http://www.apdt.co.uk

Association of Pet Behaviour Counsellors
PO BOX 46, Worcester, WR8 9YS
Telephone: 01386 751151
Fax: 01386 750743
Email: info@apbc.org.uk
Web: http://www.apbc.org.uk/

ACTIVITIES

Agility Club
http://www.agilityclub.co.uk/

British Flyball Association
PO Box 990, Doncaster, DN1 9FY
Telephone: 01628 829623
Email: secretary@flyball.org.uk
Web: http://www.flyball.org.uk/

Working Trials
Email: info@workingtrials.co.uk
Web: www.workingtrials.co.uk

World Canine Freestyle Organisation
P.O. Box 350122, Brooklyn, NY 11235-2525, USA
Telephone: (718) 332-8336
Fax: (718) 646-2686
Email: wcfodogs@aol.com
Web: www.worldcaninefreestyle.org

HEALTH

Alternative Veterinary Medicine Centre, Chinham House, Stanford in the Vale, Oxfordshire, SN7 8NQ
Telephone: 01367 710324
Fax: 01367 718243
Web: www.alternativevet.org/

Animal Health Trust
Lanwades Park, Kentford, Newmarket, Suffolk, CB8 7UU
Telephone: 01638 751000
Web: www.aht.org.uk

British Association of Veterinary Ophthalmologists (BAVO)
Email: secretary@bravo.org.uk
Web: http://www.bravo.org.uk/

British Small Animal Veterinary Association
Woodrow House, 1 Telford Way, Waterwells Business Park, Quedgeley, Gloucestershire, GL2 2AB
Telephone: 01452 726700
Fax: 01452 726701
Email: customerservices@bsava.com
Web: http://www.bsava.com/

British Veterinary Hospitals Association
Station Bungalow, Main Rd, Stocksfield, Northumberland, NE43 7HJ

Telephone: 07966 901619
Fax: 07813 915954
Email: office@bvha.org.uk
Web: http://www.bvha.org.uk/

Royal College of Veterinary Surgeons
Belgravia House, 62-64 Horseferry Road, London, SW1P 2AF
Telephone: 0207 222 2001
Fax: 0207 222 2004
Email: admin@rcvs.org.uk
Web: www.rcvs.org.uk

ASSISTANCE DOGS

Canine Partners
Mill Lane, Heyshott, Midhurst, West Sussex, GU29 0ED
Telephone: 08456 580480
Fax: 08456 580481
Web: www.caninepartners.co.uk

Dogs for the Disabled
The Frances Hay Centre, Blacklocks Hill, Banbury, Oxon, OX17 2BS
Telephone: 01295 252600
Web: www.dogsforthedisabled.org

Guide Dogs for the Blind Association
Burghfield Common, Reading, RG7 3YG
Telephone: 01189 835555
Fax: 01189 835433
Web: www.guidedogs.org.uk/

Hearing Dogs for Deaf People
The Grange, Wycombe Road, Saunderton, Princes Risborough, Bucks, HP27 9NS
Telephone: 01844 348100
Fax: 01844 348101
Web: www.hearingdogs.org.uk

Pets as Therapy
3a Grange Farm Cottages, Wycombe Road, Saunderton, Princes Risborough, Bucks, HP27 9NS
Telephone: 01845 345445
Fax: 01845 550236
Web: http://www.petsastherapy.org/

Support Dogs
21 Jessops Riverside, Brightside Lane, Sheffield, S9 2RX
Tel: 01142 617800
Fax: 01142 617555
Email: supportdogs@btconnect.com
Web: www.support-dogs.org.uk

puppy sponsor

Dogs for the Disabled

Help us turn paws into helping hands

Sponsor a **Dogs for the Disabled** puppy for just £5.00 per month and you could help change someone's life.

www.dogsforthedisabled.org   **Telephone: 01295 252600**

Dogs for the Disabled
Registered charity number: 1092960